Enterprise Relationship Management

Today's successful businesses rely on globalisation for their prosperity. The complex physical and virtual supply chain networks that support globalisation require proactive engagement, shared understanding, outcome based thinking and collaborative working. This is an insightful book that unpacks the dynamics of effective 'enterprise relationship management' and provides the reader with the tools, techniques and procedures needed to optimise twenty-first-century supply chains.
  Air Vice Marshal Graham Howard, Assistant Chief of Defence Staff (Logistics Operations)

Customers no longer demand a product or a service; they want outcomes – the fusion of different offerings – to satisfy them. Companies which are great at producing one or just a few of the things that make up these outcomes are faced with a stark choice: either develop all that is required often at eye-watering cost and risk, or partner with other organisations. The latter is increasingly the right answer but provides new challenges which demand focused attention. Enterprise Relationship Management *offers some invaluable insights into this challenging space and I commend the book to you.*
  Matt Wiles, Managing Director, Serco Defence

As an entrepreneur that has started several businesses, most of which were centred on partnerships, I can highly recommend Enterprise Relationship Management *as a real 'tour de force' of this topic. It is clear that the authors have distilled their deep knowledge and many years experience into this book. It covers 'all you need to know' of this increasingly important and often neglected corner of the modern business world. I particularly enjoyed Chapters 3 and 4 on cultural influences and found the section on reporting very helpful. Figure 6.9 is typical of the very useful graphics throughout the book and deals with the key question 'make, collaborate or buy'; increasingly the answer is 'collaborate' and this book is the perfect guide to efficiently managing that process.*
  Mike Reilly, CEO, Ether NDE Ltd

Enterprise Relationship Management

A Paradigm For Alliance Success

ANDREW HUMPHRIES and
RICHARD GIBBS

Routledge
Taylor & Francis Group

LONDON AND NEW YORK

First published in paperback 2024

First published 2015 by Gower Publishing

Published 2016 by Routledge
4 Park Squaare, Milton Park, Abingdon, Oxon OX14 4RN

and by Routledge
605 Third Avenue, New York, NY 10158

Routledge is an imprint of the Taylor & Francis Group, an informa business

Publisher's Note
The publisher has gone to great lengths to ensure the quality of this reprint but points out that some imperfections in the original copies may be apparent.

British Library Cataloguing in Publication Data
A catalogue record for this book is available from the British Library.

Library of Congress Cataloging-in-Publication Data
Humphries, Andrew, 1949–
    Enterprise relationship management : a paradigm for alliance success / by Andrew Humphries and Richard Gibbs.
        pages cm
    Includes bibliographical references and index.
    ISBN 978-1-4724-2908-7 (hardback : alk. paper) – ISBN 978-1-4724-2910-0 (ebook) – ISBN 978-1-4724-2909-4 (epub) 1. Strategic alliances (Business) I. Gibbs, Richard, 1955– II. Title.

    HD69.S8H857 2015
    658'.046–dc23

                                                                            2014031713

ISBN: 978-1-4724-2908-7 (hbk)
ISBN: 978-1-03-283712-3 (pbk)
ISBN: 978-1-315-57988-7 (ebk)

DOI: 10.4324/9781315579887

Contents

List of Figures

List of Tables

About the Authors

Dr Andrew Humphries and Dr Richard Gibbs write, lecture and consult on how firms can improve their competitive positions by improving the performance and effectiveness of their partnerships.

They have been described as 'academic practitioners', with one foot in the academic world and one firmly in the commercial world. Their work is based on independent research, exploring and uncovering the dynamics and drivers of supply chain relationships, marketing channels and strategic alliances. They have a distinctive mix of hands-on experience and theoretical reputation.

Andrew Humphries

Andrew completed a 35-year career in the UK Royal Air Force, culminating as Head of Defence Aviation Logistics. He was awarded his PhD from Cranfield School of Management, where he continues to carry out research as a Visiting Fellow. He earned his MBA from the Open University.

Andrew founded SCCI Ltd in 2004. SCCI is located in Milton Keynes, and uses a unique, powerful technique to measure the effectiveness and diagnose the improvement opportunities in collaborative business relationships. He has successfully helped to increase customer/supplier loyalty, revitalise troubled partnerships and provide performance metrics for improved governance internationally in rail, construction, manufacturing, retail, automotive, agri-food, IT outsourcing and facilities management, as well as in the defence and justice sectors.

He continues to research the subject of collaboration between organisations, and works with a number of universities in the UK, the US and Europe. He has published widely in academic journals such as the *British Journal of Management*, *European Journal of Marketing*, *International Journal of Logistics Management*, *Journal of Service Research*, *Journal of Supply Chain Management* and *International Journal of Logistics Management*. He has been featured in the *Financial Times*, has written for trade and professional magazines such as *Chief Purchasing Officer Agenda* and is a speaker at international conferences. He can be contacted at andrew.humphries@sccindex.com.

Richard Gibbs

Richard is a recognised expert in marketing channels and alliance management. He earned a PhD from the University of Gloucestershire and an MBA from Henley Management College. His career spans senior sales and marketing positions in major multinational companies such as Xerox and Novell Inc. His most recent focus has been on business transformation and change management.

Richard is a visiting lecturer at the University of Winchester. He continues to research into various aspects of inter-organisational relationships, specifically addressing how firms can gain competitive advantage through their partnerships He is an accomplished author, and has published in both the management press and academic journals. Richard can be contacted at richardkgibbs@hotmail.com.

Andrew and Richard based their previous books *Strategic Alliances and Marketing Partnerships: Gaining Competitive Advantage Through Collaboration and Partnering* (2009) and *Collaborative Change: Creating High Performance Partnerships and Alliances* (2010) on their continuing research programmes. These came together as collaborative initiatives spurred by a series of common findings and a motivation to provide operational management with a set of practical tools that would increase the likelihood of partnering excellence. This book continues in this endeavour by providing insights into their latest leading-edge knowledge and related practical experience.

Foreword

If you cannot measure relationships, you cannot manage relationships.

(Adapted from an observation of Lord Kelvin's)

Increasingly it is being recognised that companies can no longer sustain competitive advantage without effective collaboration with multiple stakeholders. These stakeholders may include suppliers, customers, government, non-governmental organisations and joint venture partners, just to name a few. Each can have a significant impact on the success or otherwise of a business. The concept of enterprise relationship management, defined as the management process for co-ordinating business activities to the success of a joint or multi-party endeavour, is essential for the success of increasing numbers of businesses today.

The recognition that competition is no longer between individual organisations, but the supply chains they are part of also emphasises the need for effective relationship management with supply chain partners. This is further emphasised by recognising the strategic goal of supply chain management, which myself and colleagues at Cranfield School of Management have identified as: to manage upstream and downstream relationships with suppliers and customers in order to create enhanced value in the final marketplace at less cost to the supply chain as a whole.

Value – those things customers and stakeholders perceive as important and beneficial – is created through relationships, both internal to the organisation and external to it. The increased awareness of the 'triple bottom line', which focuses an organisation on economic value (profits), societal value (people) and environmental value (planet), has driven organisations to build and maintain relationships in new ways. The traditional procurement philosophy of identifying suppliers that can be leveraged by driving costs and margins down, when viewed through the lens of the triple bottom line, is seen as an increasingly archaic strategy that in many instances destroys rather than creates value.

It is, however, worrying that many businesses relationships are managed and developed in an unplanned manner, with the individuals responsible for supporting business-critical relationships receiving little guidance and support. Our education system often emphasises the technical skills of operating within a business, with little time given to developing the relational skills. This, it can be argued, increases the risk profile of the organisation and its supply chain, with poor relationship management, both internally and externally, even resulting in a business failing. Many businesses have no formal process for developing, managing and exiting relationships. Few organisations have an enterprise relationship management strategy, few have documented processes and can verbalise how relationships are created and maintained. Even fewer can describe how relationships are exited in a way that all parties remain whole through 'conscious uncoupling'. It is not uncommon that when managers are asked what documentation they have which describes the approach to the relationship, they produce a legal contract which outlines the consequences of failure!

In order to manage relationships, goals need to be set and resources need to be mobilised effectively in order to achieve the goal. Measurement and monitoring become critical, and over the past fifteen years techniques have been developed to enable the measurement and monitoring of relationships from both soft and hard perspectives. Sadly, few companies set relationship goals, and even fewer measure and monitor the rich resource of relationships they have.

In order to address the above issues and formalise an approach to developing and managing business relationships both academics and practitioners have recognised the need for a more methodical approach to creating and managing collaborative relationships. It is recognised that all relationships are different but there are common building blocks and approaches to their implementation and management. Enterprise relationship management is one such approach that has been developed and provides a pragmatic, holistic methodology that can be readily adapted for all business situations. It is not just a nice idea; its principles and techniques can be applied at all levels of relationships – micro (one-to-one), macro (team-to-team) and global (enterprise-to-enterprise). Its implementation results in increased value for all stakeholders, and in my experience, cost reduction can also occur simultaneously.

This book provides an excellent overview of the tools, techniques and philosophy behind enterprise relationship management. The authors provide both managers and academics with a clear overview of the key debates and philosophies supporting the approach, sharing insights and wisdom on the development and management of business relationships. The authors, both academic practitioners, have worked for many years putting science into the measurement and management of enterprise relationships. This book highlights and emphasises the key issues that need to be explored and provides a useful outline map for navigating the complex terrain of enterprise relationship management. It complements much of our work at Cranfield School of Management, where taking academic knowledge and creating action in business is foundational to our endeavours. Particularly useful is the Bibliography at the end of the book, enabling those interested in exploring concepts in more depth to satisfy their appetites.

It will provoke a positive debate within industry and academia, but critically for practitioners, the book provides an excellent resource to enable a more formalised approach to business relationship management.

Richard Wilding OBE
Professor and Chair of Supply Chain Strategy, Cranfield School of Management.
www.som.cranfield.ac.uk/som/lscm

Introduction

This book builds on our earlier extensive research and writing. It also reflects our continued study of and engagement in the practicalities and difficulties of managing inter-organisational relationships in many forms, geographies and functional areas.

We have explored and charted the commercial and market trends over the last couple of decades, and now consider that according to Jeremy Galbreath (2002), enterprise relationship management (ERM) – 'a business strategy for value creation that is not based on cost containment, but rather on the leveraging of network-enabled processes and activities to transform the relationships between the organization and all its internal and external constituencies in order to maximize current and future opportunities' – is the best response for firms wishing to continue to delight their customers, offer meaningful jobs for their staff, and satisfy the requirements of their shareholders and broader society and the environment.

The underlying notion of ERM is that the twenty-first-century enterprise or corporation is best served when it recognises itself not as a stand-alone or siloed organisation with fixed and defined boundaries, but fluidly as a collection of relationships between core team individuals (employees of the firm) and a host of contracted staff, outsourced agencies and third-party suppliers, as well as both upstream and downstream partners. To paraphrase Professor Martin Christopher, it is no longer individual firms that compete, but interconnected organisations, to the extent that these relationships form a network of companies that will compete together in the marketplace.

The competitive advantage in the form of market offering these networks create will become ever more transient, fleeting and temporary. The unstoppable charge of technological change, globalisation and creative innovation conspires against most, if not all, advantages, being able to be copied and surpassed. The core competence of the firm can no longer be limited to the resources, assets or know-how that created this temporary benefit, but must lie in the organisation's ability to form, manage, retire and then exit partnerships while simultaneously constantly seeking out and forming new relationships.

These new relationships can then give rise to new forms of superior, albeit temporary, offerings.

The fragmented aspect of the extended enterprise means that the establishment of ways of working or organisational culture within a developing and evolving network of firms will be very difficult. Psychologist Bruce Tuckman's concept of 'forming, storming, norming, and performing' as the stages of team development (Tuckman 1965) therefore becomes increasingly relevant in the understanding of inter-organisational collaborative endeavours. It can no longer be assumed, if it ever could, that the individuals and firms involved will share any social, political or organisational cultural values and beliefs. Indeed, given the global economy, it is more likely that at least one party will be from a culture that is significantly different according to the GLOBE research country clusters and leadership preferences (House et al. 2000).

ERM has therefore morphed from being a strategic reality and necessity to being an operational practice. Firms – successful firms – must now place great stress on developing, acquiring and nurturing the skills that are required to optimise business-to-business relationships.

The emergence of effective relationship managers cannot be left to chance or best efforts. The complexity of the task, the uncertainty of the activity and the risk (benefit) associated with a successful outcome mean that firms must adopt a thoroughly professional approach. This means ensuring that there is a formal and structured process in place, attuned to delivering operational excellence, which is managed through the use and application of key metrics.

World-class ERM requires the application of both hard and soft approaches in the exactly the same manner as successful change management.

Hard tangible results which impact profit and loss (P+L), balance sheet or key processes are important. It is important to weigh and measure the value of the benefits generated and captured from any relationship or partnership. However, the adoption of a relationship management paradigm means that firms also need to seek to manage and appraise factors such as trust and commitment.

We now envisage ERM as a formal management discipline rather than an ad hoc collection of anecdotes, experiences and best practices – an established process based on proven methodologies and known success criteria that guide the relationship manager through a series of well-defined phases and stages.

The evolution of concepts in the last ten years alone has been very rewarding. When we first started to research in this area, the best business practice you would encounter came from the buyer-side key account management approach. We then witnessed the enlightening work of John Gattorna in supply chain management (see, for example, Gattorna 2006). We saw advances in thought and deed through the work of the US-based Association of Strategic Alliance Professionals, and in Europe, the tireless evangelism of Mike Nevin (see, for example, Nevin 2014). Today, we can see relational governance concepts being interwoven with contract management through the works of forward-thinking practitioners such as Tim Cummins of the International Association of Contract and Commercial Management.

Going forward, the importance of ERM will continue to grow. Indeed, the continual advances of information technology (IT) will only increase the opportunities for individuals and organisations to collaborate on a global basis. The notion of the single, monolithic enterprise epitomised by Ford Motor Company in the 1930s is long gone. The end of the large-scale multinational is nowhere in sight, but nevertheless we are witnessing the growth of myriad partners, clusters and networks as firms and individuals continue to seek advantages and benefits for their customers. For multinational companies, this will represent a challenge to fuse and optimise collaborative working with smaller and more agile firms, as well as larger corporations like themselves, and all of this on a truly international basis.

We have structured this book to provide a narrative flow reflecting and expanding on the points we have touched on above, which have been informed through the discussions in many workshops and conference sessions with managers of all disciplines.

Chapter 1 details the factors and trends that have accelerated the academic and management interest in inter-organisational relationships. It positions outsourcing and partnering as the organisational standard or norm. It proposes the notion that competitive advantage will reside in inter-organisational routines and processes and the ability of managers to leverage them.

Chapter 2 dissects the important aspects of internal and external complexity as well as the risk elements of dyadic partnerships, networks, clusters and intricate multi-path supply chains and channel to market. It introduces and describes in detail strategies that firms can adopt and operationalise to mitigate these complicating risk factors.

Chapter 3 describes the multiple layers of social, political and organisational culture which form the environment in which ERM operates. Chapter 4 then looks at the operational implications of culture, with particular reference to leadership styles and the newer studies of the GLOBE research.

Chapter 5 is a pivotal point in our book because it combines transactional exchange theory with a relational exchange perspective to describe the key drivers of partnership success and failure. It then provides a practical and very operational model to explain the cycle of events that generates high-performance partnerships, or alternatively, failing relationships.

In Chapter 6 we demonstrate the importance of applying the basic principles of scorecards and key metrics to relationship appraisal, whether in pairs of partners, consortia and at the strategic level, or in relationship portfolios. It provides a step-by-step guide on how the strengths and weakness of relationships can be measured and understood. It then shows how this knowledge can be used to stimulate the adoption of performance improvements and a continuous improvement ethos. We also show how relationship appraisal can be used as a governance measure to track performance over time. Finally, for those interested in technicalities, we touch on the science of our approach to relationship appraisal.

Chapter 7 investigates and describes the current growing phenomenon of how global organisations are evolving outsourcing and facilities management relationships from cost reduction to value creation. These relationships are typically the closest it is possible to encounter, hence there are important lessons for all collaborating organisations. We suggest that despite the apparent maturity of this business activity, getting on now for 20 years, ERM mistakes are still being made that significantly reduce firms' ability to create and capture collaborative value. We introduce the idea of a Continuous Value Creation (CVC) Cycle and use some global case studies to demonstrate how some blue-chip companies have broken their CVC Cycles. We conclude that effective ERM is the solution.

ERM involves the formal management of those aspects of a joint enterprise that contribute to the bottom line by blending together framework contracting and relational governance. Chapter 8 describes the principles of how this can be done in a structured, repeatable fashion. It extends the relationship management ideas explored earlier in the book by building the case and exploring the payback from a professional, experienced, senior function in every collaborating organisation. It explains the roles and functions of the relationship managers (RMs) who have the lead in operationalising ERM for their respective organisations. We show how the Enterprise Relationship Management Plan, which is the key information focus for a collaborative relationship, enables relationship synergy, from choosing a partner through successful operations to satisfactory dissolution.

In Chapter 9 we build on these principles by describing the practical steps that RMs can take to steer their collaborative enterprises through the Decision, Operations and Exit Phases of ERM. We also consider the essential role played by performance management, and include examples of operational score cards using the traffic light approach based upon our relationship dynamics spirals.

In Chapter 10 we describe the eight partnership types that our extensive international research has uncovered. In concert with our relationship appraisals based upon dynamic behaviour spirals, partnerships must constantly strive to maintain their forward momentum. The Gibbs + Humphries Partnering Types model essentially offers a powerful strategic perspective, but the archetypes also provide operational managers with an unusually clear insight into and understanding of the characteristics of partnerships and how organisations can react and respond appropriately to various stimuli.

The final chapter looks forward and speculates on how we see enterprise relationship management progressing and developing. Should it become the core competence of the future? We speculate on the critical importance that the extended enterprise will play in all of our lives as globalisation and technology trends enable and necessitate collaboration between otherwise independent organisations. As a key contingent factor, we consider the important, evolving roles of contractual and relational governance in ERM by answering the controversial question: 'Are contracts the enemy of good relationships?' We conclude that successful relationship management is dependent on the integration of adaptable framework contracts with factors such as openness, honesty, trust, co-operation and long-term orientation within the ERM discipline.

At the end of the book we have included two appendices whose purpose is to offer greater insight, illustration and detail to support the main ideas we have put forward. Appendix 1 is a case study that describes the relationship between Xerox and Fuji Xerox. This remains one of the most remarkable, durable and adaptive partnering examples that offers many lessons for those wishing to utilise the full force of ERM in their alliances and partnerships. Appendix 2 provides some of the detailed science that underpins the development and use of the Gibbs + Humphries Partnering Types. Taken as a whole, it provides a comprehensive view of the wide range of critical facets that make up inter-organisational relationship management.

Some of the material used in the book has previously appeared as 'white papers' on the SCCI website or in lectures. We have consolidated and developed this work to bring together our latest thinking. We wish to thank Linda McComie in particular for her permission to reproduce material she has worked on with Andrew.

Chapter 1
The Extended Organisation

Introduction

The topic of outsourcing, partnerships and collaboration has become a regular feature on management agendas and in the business press, as well as a hot topic of academic interest. Indeed, many newer organisational forms are structured around outsourced arrangements of one kind or another, while hitherto traditionally structured corporations are morphing into extended enterprises. At the same time, firms proudly announce the developments and offspring from their various alliances and partnerships. This chapter tracks the trends and reasons why collaborative working of whatever kind has become so popular and prevalent. It looks at the academic theories that explored and then supported the rationale for the fragmentation of the enterprise and the growth of partnering. It also describes the commercial realities that presaged the necessity of seeking competitive advantage beyond the firm's boundaries. The pace and momentum of these commercial realities – namely, rapid technological advancement and globalisation with the consequential need for innovation and change – show no indication of abating. This opening chapter sheds light on the theory behind the practice as well as the practice behind the theory, revealing the changes from firms as islands of activity to firms as networks of dependencies and interdependencies.

Twenty-first-century Threats and Opportunities

In December 1999, one of the dominant stories in the business press concerned the anticipated end of the civilised world.

The old century ended with apocalyptic fears concerning the 'Millennium Bug' causing mass disruption of the financial and banking network, with planes falling out of the sky and total gridlock on the roads in major cities.[1] The Millennium Bug (more simply referred to as the 'Y2K Bug') was a result of using two digits (not four) to represent a year, so that 01 was interpreted as 1901 and 00 as 1900. This seemed fine and dandy in the 1950s when software protocols and programs were being defined. When the rollover from 1999 to 2000 occurred, there was a fear that software programs would not be able to deal with the confusion caused by the two digits (did they refer to 1900 or 2000?).

Programs which had an event window or horizon would simply 'bomb out' – 'I know your contract runs to 2001, but, according to my time clock, it's 1900 and I am shutting down.'

There were some minor hiccoughs, such as in Colonie, New York State, where a man was given a $91,250 fine for returning a video 100 years overdue, or the newborn Danish baby whose computer records showed him to be 100 years old.

Apart from such occurrences, the Millennium Bug seems to have been a minor blessing for IT firms. It created the level of boardroom interest that was galvanised into action, which was converted into consultancy and hardware (backup) sales. After the (non-)event, the deferred business-as-normal IT investment by companies then slowly started up again.

The January 2000 edition of the *Harvard Business Review* carried an article by Prahalad and Ramaswamy entitled 'Co-opting Customer Competence', in which they wrote: 'Major discontinuities such as deregulation, globalisation, technology convergence and the rapid revolution of the internet have blurred the roles that companies plan in their dealing with other businesses.'

According to Prahalad and Ramaswamy, these external pressures and factors which were encouraging a shift away from well-defined roles of firms, supplies and customers to a world where traditional hands-off relationships and boundaries became blurred or effectively disappeared completely.

The Y2K Bug and the intense collaborative work with customers to solve the anticipated technical and global problems provided a timely illustration of their point.

---

1   Leeds, J. (2000) 'Year 2000 Bug Triggers Few Disruptions', *Los Angeles Times*, 4 January: http://articles.latimes.com/2000/jan/04/business/fi-50565 (accessed 14 December 2013).

From a Tactical Option to a Way of Working

Nearly two decades earlier, it had been external pressures and factors that occupied Michael Porter's thinking in his book *Competitive Strategy* (1998). Porter's seminal work focused on the impact the industry structure would have on determining a firm's ability to earn above-average profits. His Five Forces Model was – and in some locations, probably still is – the starting point for many MBA students.

Porter's five forces include three forces from 'horizontal' competition: the threat of substitute products or services, the threat of established rivals, and the threat of new entrants. The two forces from 'vertical' competition are the bargaining power of suppliers and the bargaining power of customers.

This five forces analysis is just one element of the Porter's strategic modelling of a firm and its environment. The other elements in the model are the value chain (another business concept that is still relevant) and the generic strategies. Porter distilled business strategies into three fundamental options, which covered cost leadership, differentiation and market segmentation (or focus). The realities of change in the decades since Porter first wrote have been intense.

The world in 1985 was socially and politically different from today. The Berlin Wall fell in 1989, heralding the end of the Cold War, and the subsequent expansion of the European market created a new, substantial economic entity of 28 states, representing around 20 per cent of the world's nominal GDP. In the 1990s, Manmohan Singh, the former Indian Finance Minister, opened up the sub-continent such that India now represents the strategic hothouse of the world's technology companies. Silicon Valley has now spiritually relocated to Bangalore. The transfer of sovereignty of Hong Kong to the People's Republic of China in 1997, the entry of China into the World Trade Organization in 2001 and the 2008 Beijing Olympic Games signalled the opening up of the Chinese market to the rest of the world.

Technological change has been equally radical and disruptive. Prahalad and Ramaswamy argued that the Internet would be a prime driver and enabler to the co-option of customers into the firm's set of networked competences, but they were writing before the explosion of social media. According to Wikipedia (established in 2001), which itself has 365 million readers worldwide and 71,000 active editors, in 2013 there were 1.3 billion users on Facebook, 800 million unique YouTube users a month and 200 million on Twitter. This unheralded explosion of interconnectedness has created a massive opportunity for communication between customers, suppliers and firms. In particular, many firms are now accelerating the use of social media to fuel the innovation pipeline. Notwithstanding this encouraging trend, social media remain in many instances peripheral to hard-wired, traditional processes for innovation, query management and customer feedback.

Resources, Skills and Competences

In contrast to Porter's external focus, an alternative school of thought began to emerge in the 1990s that adopted a different perspective. Academic strategists like Barney (1991) and Rumelt (1991) shifted the attention away from an external analysis of a firm's environment and the associated competitive pressures to an internal appraisal of the firm's ability to use what it has in such a way as to outperform its competitors.

This second school was erected around the pillars of the resources and competencies a firm had at its disposal. These resources are considered as tradable, generic assets that can be divided into three categories: tangible (infrastructure, natural resources and money), intangible (image, reputation, markets and brands) and human (experts). These resources and competences are also seen as being unique to the firm, and in contrast to Porter's position, are viewed as significantly heterogeneous, and are likely to be so over time. Indeed, forces such as imperfect mobility, imitability and substitutability are likely to keep them that way and prevent resources, and therefore firms, from becoming homogeneous. This means that in contrast to Porter's position, no two firms will possess the same resources in the same quantity or degree of competence, and critically, a competitive firm seeking to enjoy or usurp the benefits of these resources will discover that they are not easy to acquire, either through transference or because of their relative scarcity in the marketplace.

All of this means that rather than being defined by its competitive environment, a firm's competitive advantage will be bounded by the resources it has available to deploy. As such, this line of strategic thinking has encouraged firms to seek out, develop and then protect additional and incremental resources. As a consequence, many firms began to look beyond the boundaries of their own operations, realising that an increase in their resources could be accomplished through mergers and acquisitions or through joint venture and the formation of strategic alliances (see Figure 1.1).

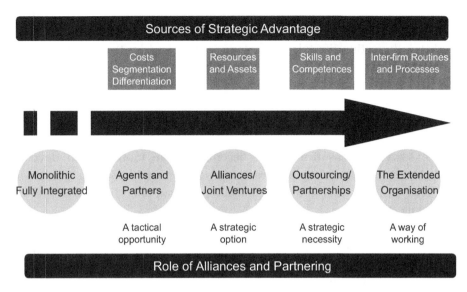

Figure 1.1   Strategy trends and drivers of the extended organisation

Prahalad and Hamel (1998) extended and expanded on this line of thinking. They considered that it is not solely the physical or tangible resources a firm possesses that frame its competitive advantage; the skills and abilities – the competences – of a firm to effectively deploy its resources give it an edge in the marketplace.

Therefore, if resources are the 'things' a firm has available to use, its competences are the skills and know-how to use them. Competences are, almost by definition, distinctive and unique to the firm, as well as hard to imitate. They take time to develop, and need considerable care and expertise to amass and subsequently leverage. Competences can take many forms, such as organising, R&D, selling and team-working abilities. They are also likely to be drawn from across an organisation's functional units, and thus extend into human resources, financial management, organisational development, technology development and implementation, to create unique bundles of capabilities from across the broadest spectrum of the firm's interests. Once a firm has recognised and identified what it is good at, then managerial expertise needs to be applied to create and deploy these competences as a sustainable source of advantage for the firm.

Initially there was an upsurge in patents (registration and litigation) as firms sought to document and protect their potential advantages. This was followed by cross-licensing arrangements between firms that spurred new sectors such as 'edutainment' (education + entertainment) as well as reinvigorating the PC market and creating lifestyle technology (epitomised by the iPhone, and of course, the iPad).

The Growth of Alliances and Outsourcing

At the same time, as firms were becoming more motivated to develop competences, there was a parallel trend that saw companies looking to leverage their relationships with external organisations and suppliers both up and down the supply chain.

In the 1980s, new organisational structures were seen to be emerging that were based less on vertical hierarchies and market-based processes and more on administrative processes and negotiation. This coming together of firms into partnering relationships can be seen as coincidental to changing market conditions. The accelerated pace of technological change and global competition has been associated with rising customer expectations, the fall of product-based differentiation and raised standards of operational performance. This meant that the earlier building blocks of competitive advantage were no longer viable, and firms were forced to look elsewhere for new features and functionality to delight their customers.

The rapid increase in the number of alliances in the 1980s was matched by the growing awareness of the complexity of managing such relationships as firms began to report increasing failures and mortality. The estimate that around 60 per cent of such partnerships were failing to meet their objectives was a possible contributing factor to the levelling out in the growth of these organisational structures. The 1990s, however, saw continued and growing competitive pressures coupled with ever-rising costs of R&D and shortened product life cycle; these factors encouraged firms to turn back to collaborative technology alliances as a strategic necessity.

Two academics, Professors Quinn and Hilmer, explained and reinforced this necessity, as well as joining together the various strands of strategic thinking and commercial trends:

> *Two new strategic approaches, when properly combined, allow managers to leverage their company's skills and resources well beyond levels available in other strategies. Firstly, concentrate the firm's own resources on a set of core competencies where it can achieve definable*

pre-eminence and provide unique value to customers. Secondly, strategically outsource other activities, including many traditionally considered integral to any company, for which the company has neither a critical strategic need nor special capabilities.

(Quinn and Hilmer 1994)

Firms reinvigorated their exploration of the benefits of outsourcing elements of their operations to third parties. Firms would undertake 'make or buy' analyses to determine whether there was more value in retaining ownership of an activity in-house in comparison to buying in the service from an external organisation.

Oliver Williamson's transaction cost economics ideas constitute one of the most important management paradigms that explains the reasons for this phenomenon and aids the understanding of the mechanics of firms working collaboratively. As firms look at ways to reduce or strip out costs from their business, an analysis of the value chain reveals that certain primary activities are key to the business; these are its competences. Where the firm has a unique capacity or capability, it makes sense to continue to keep this in-house. But where the activity is less central to the business, an evaluation can be made as to whether it is more cost-effective to engage a third party to perform the task. This is the 'make or buy' decision that many firms call 'investment appraisal'.

For many firms, manufacturing and sales activities were among the first candidates to be outsourced to other organisations. It can be considered that the use of marketing channels or intermediaries to undertake the selling activity spurred the dynamic growth in the IT sector. The direct selling giants such as IBM and Digital were able to flex their own selling muscles into the corporate accounts, while the smaller and younger organisations such as Novell, Microsoft and Compaq used specialised resellers to reach the lucrative small and medium enterprise market.

This trend wasn't limited to the IT sector. The clothing company Benetton was the archetypal exponent of creating a value chain of capabilities. Its manufacturers were all part-time, contracted out, and its retailers were mainly franchises. Benetton provided the just-in-time logistics system, the garment finishing/warehousing, the branding/market positioning and advertising, as well as pioneering use of electronic point of sale-fed information systems. This proved to be a winning combination that was, at the time, very hard to imitate. Nike Inc., the US-based sports company, was another early example of the virtual enterprise where information systems have been used to co-ordinate each step of its far-flung activities, from material sourcing and manufacturing through to marketing and retailing. In Chapter 7 we will explore in more detail the problems of capturing value in outsourcing relationships.

The Extended Organisation

Davis and Spekman, among others, began to speak about the extended enterprise and collaborative supply chains:

> *The extended enterprise is the entire set of both upstream and downstream collaborating companies, from raw materials to end-use consumption, that work together to bring value to the market place. Its primary goal is to leverage the skills/capabilities of its members to achieve a sustainable competitive advantage relative to other competing supply chain networks.*
>
> *(Davis and Spekman 2003)*

Globalisation and technology have been both drivers and enablers of the development of the external extensions to the organisation incorporating clusters and networks of collaborating firms.

These extensions include upstream as well downstream activities. Commercial pressures have moved the supply chain from the dark days of lowest-cost procurement to collaborative, complex and integrated teams, to the extent that Professor Martin Christopher suggests it is now possible to envisage that 'we no longer compete as individual companies, we compete as supply chains'.[2]

The US automotive industry, for example, is typically characterised by testosterone-fuelled negotiations, but under the charismatic leadership of Tom Stallkamp, Chrysler changed the rules (at least until its acquisition by Daimler). Chrysler's SCORE programme developed closer working relationships with its suppliers, incentivised them for their performance, shared cost savings with them and brought them generally closer to the production and development activities.

---

2   Cranfield School of Management (2007) 'Interview: Professor Martin Christopher. Logistics and
     Supply Chain Management: Creating Value Added Networks'. Bedford: Cranfield School of
     Management: www.som.cranfield.ac.uk/som/dinamic-content/media/knowledgeinterchange/
     booksummaries/Logistics%20and%20Supply%20Chain%20Management/Transcript.pdf
     (accessed 21 June 2012).

The savings that SCORE generated for Chrysler amounted to billions of dollars over an extended period.

In the IT sector, Dell's early success was underpinned by the closeness of the relationships with its suppliers and the approach taken in their management. A fundamental plank of Michael Dell's original strategy was the belief that it was better to partner with suppliers of PC parts and components rather than to integrate backward and get into parts and components manufacturing in its own right. Dell can identify several benefits it gained through its approach. It adopted a limited supplier strategy, and worked only with those firms that could demonstrate leadership in technology, which led to enhanced quality and performance of Dell's PCs. Dell made a commitment to each supplier that it would purchase a specified percentage of its requirements from each. This meant that in an often turbulent marketplace, Dell was practically guaranteed to get the components it needed, when and where it needed them. Dell invited its suppliers into its product development process, which meant that they were on hand during critical launch periods to resolve any technical or quality issues. Dell provided its suppliers with a 'window' into the manufacturing or assembly process so that they could better plan their own production. Dell shared critical information with its suppliers on a real-time basis. A monthly forecast was complemented by a closed information loop that provided Dell's manufacturing with product availability details and its suppliers with the 'pull' or demand on parts. This was not an arm's length relationship, and although suppliers might not appreciate the high levels of service that Dell expected, they could not argue that they did not understand or appreciate the key metrics of performance required of them.

Tomorrow's Differentiated Competitive Advantage

Firms (and managers) which want to be successful over the coming decade will need to recognise that the strategic pillars that supported earlier corporate development and performance have simply been torn down.

As illustrated in the framework of value creation shown in Table 1.1, customer value was previously defined in terms of the dimensions of product quality/price factors, physical distribution factors, and service and support. In a world of rapid transition and shortening life cycles, these dimensions become the hygiene factors, and as such, typically cannot be relied upon to provide all of the value that customers are looking for.

Table 1.1   Framework of value creation

Product/quality/price factors	Physical distribution factors	Service and support factors
Reliable, high-quality product	Efficient distribution facility management	Pre-sale support
Competitive pricing	Rapid and accurate order processing	Post-sale support, including fix, repair and replace
Profitable product	Cost-efficient inventory management	
Product line availability	Rapid and reliable delivery	
Substantive guarantees	Timely restocking and rotation	
Innovative, technologically advanced design	Sufficient distribution coverage	
New/improvement product cycle		
Rapid response to competition		

Today and over the next few years, customer value lies in human interaction, personalisation of service offerings and fluidity of transactions. As such, creative insight, flexibility and personal chemistry become more important than rules and processes.

In order to deliver this level and type of value, firms will need to maintain accelerated change and rapid innovation to keep ahead of the pack.

In recent years, technology has inspired entirely new industries and has fundamentally and structurally changed others. Advances in alternative energy, biotechnology, nanotechnology and other fields beyond IT continue to revolutionise products, operations and business models. Companies will have to learn how to adopt the benefits quickly and efficiently, and then move on to the next big thing, minimising disruption on the way. The pace and extent of this change and innovation bestow mixed blessings. Such speed and complexity can bring with them a sense of uneasiness as managers struggle to understand the new products or the business they find themselves in, and the effects of the dynamic nature of change can be likened to vertigo.

The new 'social' change of Facebook, Twitter and so on, as well as the ubiquity of the tablet and smartphone (for example, the iPad and iPhone), are having a profound effect on communication – personal, commercial, social and political. Hand in glove with these devices, new technologies are enabling companies to 'mine' and understand the 'big data' this digital storm is creating.

While incremental product innovation and global expansion have historically been the main drivers of growth for companies, the current phase of development is business model innovation which is gaining momentum within the context of today's low-growth, resource-constrained world. A strong understanding of customers' broader, personalised and customised transactional and consumption experiences needs must be combined with better access to talent and technologies on a global basis to successfully innovate and unlock growth. This shift – subtle, but seismic at the same time – will represent the basis of the innovation strategy over the next couple of years.

The world has become more connected and more accessible, which presents heightened competition, but also opportunities. It goes without saying that firms will need to capitalise on the relative economic growth rates around the world, but firms will equally need to optimise their cost structure on a global basis, leveraging the benefits of resources and labour cost arbitrage. Raw materials and lower wages become an entry point, as companies also need to explore, identify and then utilise skills and resources that are located outside their domestic markets. CEOs see tremendous opportunities to expand their global reach, tapping into new sources of expertise and new markets. The polarisation between home market and overseas will need to be broken down as organisations are challenged to act in an integrated manner on a global basis.

Change and Adapt, or Go Extinct

All of this means that technological changes plus globalisation put pressure on traditional business models. The hard reality is that 'The business model that has sustained us for decades is no longer sufficient to sustain profitability,' stated Bill Ford of Ford Motor Company in 2006,[3] echoing Xerox's former CEO, Anne Mulcahy's statement that 'Xerox's business model is unsustainable.'[4] 'The memory business model is broken,' according to Darrell Rinerson, Chairman, President and CEO of Unity Semiconductor Corp.[5] Irrespective of the industry sector, from finance through to heavy manufacturing, firms around the world are recognising that they need to

---

3   'Ford Names New CEO', CNN Money, 5 September 2006: http://money.cnn.com/2006/09/05/news/companies/ford/ (accessed 6 September 2014).
4   'America's Best Leaders: Anne Mulcahy, Xerox CEO', *U.S. News & World Report*, 19 November 2008: www.usnews.com/news/best-leaders/articles/2008/11/19/americas-best-leaders-anne-mulcahy-xerox-ceo (accessed 6 September 2014).
5   Mark LaPedus, 'Exec: Memory Business Model is Broken', *EE Times*, 25 June 2009: www.eetimes.com/document.asp?doc_id=1171251 (accessed 6 September 2014).

overhaul and revamp critical elements of their structure and finance model. New business designs are needed that facilitate faster and more extensive collaboration on a worldwide scale and allow rapid reconfiguration when new opportunities appear.

Eli Lilly is a recognised leader in pharmaceuticals and drug development. The pharma sector is confronted with some harsh realities:

- R&D productivity has fallen in recent years, with a decrease in the number of approvals for new molecular entities and biologics.
- R&D costs continue to rise, amounting to billions of dollars per approval.
- Patent expirations peak, creating a 'leaking' of revenue and profit.
- An ageing population and rising health costs for governments put pressure on the drug companies to perform.

Eli Lilly is one of a number of drug companies pioneering a collaborative innovation model. It has moved from positioning itself as a fully integrated pharmaceutical company (FIPCO) to a fully integrated pharmaceutical network (FIPNet). The FIPCO model ensured that everything from development through to marketing was contained within one company. This meant that it was safe, secure and guaranteed quality, but was insufficient and ineffective in meeting today's challenges.

Eli Lilly has now reached out beyond its organisational boundaries to develop relationships with firms that can provide it with the rapid and accelerated innovation it requires to stay ahead in its sector. The company has formed a risk- and reward-sharing alliance with Nicholas Piramal India Limited (NPIL). Under this contract, NPIL will develop one of Lilly's molecules at its own expense, from pre-clinical work to early clinical trials.

If NPIL is successful and the compound reaches the second stage of human testing, Lilly can reacquire it in exchange for certain milestone payments and royalties.

These collaborative business models offer several benefits, including reducing costs, increasing development capacity, accelerating the drug development process, along with better leverage of Lilly's assets as well as those of its external partners.

Lilly's FIPNet strategy aims to bring together three critical components, independent of source:

- creativity;
- capacity and capability;
- capital and risk management.

A high percentage of compounds previously wholly synthesised by Eli Lilly chemists are now synthesised by third parties, the most significant being a Chinese company called ShangPharma whose productivity is greater than Eli Lilly's own record of accomplishment.

The critical proof of concept stage in drug development and testing is the crossover point where clear evidence of a drug's efficacy on humans needs to be gathered. This is now done using a global network of scientists, saving Eli Lilly millions of dollars and shortening the time to the approval stage.

At the same time, the Lilly Phenotypic Drug Discovery Initiative (PD^2 – pronounced 'PD squared') uses Lilly-developed disease-state arrays with a secure Web portal to enable universities and biotechnology laboratories to submit compounds for therapeutic evaluation.[6] The Web portal allows these institutions to submit confidentially the structure of the compound, which if it meets the required criteria, is followed by the submission of physical samples for biological testing. Eli Lilly will then provide the research team with a broad assessment of the compound's biological profile against four critical areas (Alzheimer's disease, cancer, diabetes and osteoporosis). During this process, the intellectual property rights remain with the research institution and Eli Lilly reserves the primary right to negotiate a collaborative or licensing agreement.

William Chin, VP of Discovery Research and Clinical Investigation at Lilly, says: 'We believe open collaboration with a network of scientists will create new venues to deepen our understanding of complex biological processes and eventually to discover novel therapeutics that benefit patients.'

FIPNet represents a new organisational structure, the development of new processes and a drive for innovation that relies on initiatives that cross the organisational divide.

---

6   Eli Lilly (2009) 'Eli Lilly and Company Announces New Drug Discovery Initiative'. Press release, 15 June: https://investor.lilly.com/releasedetail.cfm?ReleaseID=389589 (accessed 14 December 2013).

Conclusions

Globalisation and technology advancement continue to be the drivers for process change, innovation and business model restructuring. These are not trends that seem likely to slow down in the coming years. It is clear that leveraging the benefits of globalisation will necessitate firms working more collaboratively with other organisations. Equally assured is that the source of creativity and innovation lies in extended forms of organisation where design and technology enable the necessary communication and control. Nevertheless, the challenge that is now confronting firms is that the source of competitive advantage might not just be in the creation of these extended architectures or in the access to resources and expertise; it might be far more subtle.

The ability of firms to realise the benefits of their collaborative relationships will be dependent on how well they manage inter-firm routines and processes.

To manage these routines and processes and to release the potential they offer, organisations will need to develop the understanding, skills and processes that will enable them to build effective relationships with external, independent firms, along with management structures to make it happen (see Table 1.2). Therefore, it is not the relationships themselves but the ability to manage them, leverage them and learn from them that become the sources of competitive advantage.

As we sped through the first decade of the new millennium and encountered a global recession, it became abundantly clear that no firm had the resources and competencies in-house to compete effectively in the new world market. Constellations or networks of firms will need to work together and compete against other constellations, since a firm that stands alone most likely will fail alone. The notion has become increasingly well established that partnering with other firms and outsourcing of previously internally managed activities are no longer options or even strategic directions, but simply an accepted way of working.

Table 1.2   Strategic trends and corporate options

	Technology	**Globalisation**	**Business model**
Change	Adopting the benefits Minimising the disruption	Optimising the costs Integrating the world	Quality management. process re-engineering
Innovate	Developing and deploying the latest technology	Developing and accessing new markets	New offering development
Collaborate	Reaching for the future	Reaching for the world	Extended corporation

In the next chapter we will talk about the implications for management of operating with and within the highly complex networks of business relationships that are commonplace in both the private and public sectors.

Chapter 2

The Complex Challenges of Collaboration Management

Introduction

Most of us understand the difficulties of managing the complex web of relationships that exist within large and small organisations. The need to co-ordinate the activities of the different parts, getting Commercial to talk to Operations and expecting IT to consult with anyone are just a few of the problems that get even harder if you have people spread around the world. But at least you have a corporate culture, a system of governance and common information systems that can ease the pain. At the end of the day, someone with the appropriate power can bang heads together and say, 'We will do it this way.' This is not the case when managing relationships between businesses and organisations. Independently minded entities which are used to making their own decisions, devising their own strategies and relishing their freedom deciding to team up with others seems perverse. This is especially true when the objective is to step into the unknown and trust a partner to help to create an output that none of them could achieve independently.

The clash of cultures is only the start. As shown in Figure 2.1, governance, communications, processes, structure, people and change all add up to an exponential increase in management complexity. Furthermore, few organisations enter into these alliances with appropriate success strategies, and most of them seriously underestimate the increased level of management effort needed. On top of this, the environment has the ability to throw spanners into the works without warning, which can spell potential disaster or golden opportunity.

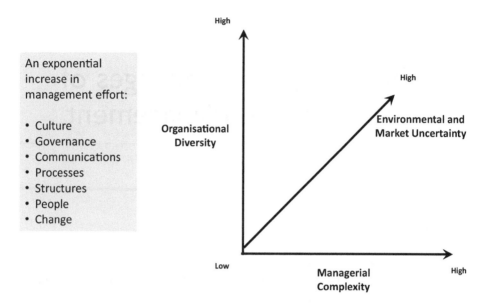

Figure 2.1   The drivers of relationship management complexity

Living with Complexity

As espoused in Darwin's theories of evolution in the natural world, companies and organisations must adapt and change in order to survive. Social, technical, economic and political developments in their environment, often perceived through changes in the market, will affect them externally and internally. Given the way ends are so often achieved these days by partnering, 'alliancing' and forming networks, achieving adaptation through collaborative change is a crucial competence alongside firms' traditional resources and capabilities. We use the word 'crucial' because getting it wrong can have very serious implications. Studies on the organisational and environmental factors that led to technical failures which resulted in the *Columbia* space shuttle disaster coined the term 'interactive complexity'. Multiple interdependencies, non-linear feedback and hidden consequences can occur within tightly coupled systems where there is little slack or room for manoeuvre. Thus, actions in one part of the system directly and immediately affect other parts, and may fall outside the system's usual capacity to catch and correct errors. The loss of the *Columbia* in 2003 was not just a failure of NASA, but also a failure of its network of contractor organisations and its stakeholder environment.

Complex organisational relationships might be defined as systems of interconnected autonomous entities that make choices to survive, and as collectives, their relationship systems evolve and self-organise over time. Self-organisation involves a process in which new structures, patterns and properties emerge spontaneously. Those managers who are only comfortable when they feel they are in complete control will find this a frightening prospect.

An illustration of adaptive firm behaviour concerns three big players in a cellular telephone supply network. It highlights the different approaches that Nokia and Ericsson took when a fire disrupted supplies from Philips, the sole supplier for a particular chip common to both manufacturers. While Ericsson suffered an estimated $2.34 billion loss, Nokia engaged directly with Philips to restore supply using alternative supply options. It modified designs of the handsets where possible and secured worldwide manufacturing capacity from Philips to ensure a steady supply of the chips. Meanwhile, the direct interaction between top management of Nokia and Philips further enhanced the ability of Nokia to adapt in the future.

Complex adaptive systems are evident wherever you look, and almost every aspect of modern life is dependent on multiple organisations working closely together to deliver their outputs. Furthermore, whether it is the loaf of bread one buys from a supermarket, the immunisation injection one receives from a doctor or the cell phone we could not live without, all rely on complex design, manufacture, training, IT, logistics and marketing. These systems must also change as end user/customer needs change, either as a result of fashion-led demand or as a result of public policy. This is the nature of complex relationship management – ERM.

External Complexity Factors

Whether through developments like global warming, failure in the financial markets or changes in regulatory policy, the external environment has an almost unlimited capacity to affect and surprise business networks. In this section, we will concentrate on how collaborative organisations react to these external changes.

Many use the terms 'uncertainty' and 'complexity' synonymously when talking about firms' difficulties in predicting how future environments will influence their own well-being. Uncertainty is multidimensional, caused by rapid changes in the environment, by changes in the dynamic elements that make up the environment, and by difficulty in predicting how best to deal with them. Rapid changes weaken the cause–effect relationship, leading to an increase in the absence of patterns and making it difficult for managers to rely on history and experience to make decisions. Uncertainty may affect individual firms or be system-wide, and will result in a variety of relationship-building and network re-configuring behaviours as they seek to mitigate risks and enhance their positions. Firms may also act offensively or defensively, depending on their strategic orientation or in response to specific external stimuli.

Firm-specific uncertainty is unique and often internal to a firm, but within its means to control – for example, entering a new market, acquiring another firm, turnover in top management, technical uncertainty about the likelihood of a new technology's success and the associated costs and uncertainty in relationships with existing partners. These events can be destabilising to existing collaborative relationships and may derail current change initiatives and projects. Some partners may start to loosen their ties and begin looking for other partners. An affected firm may attempt to strengthen its own network of relationships in the hope that collective support will help it to weather its difficulties.

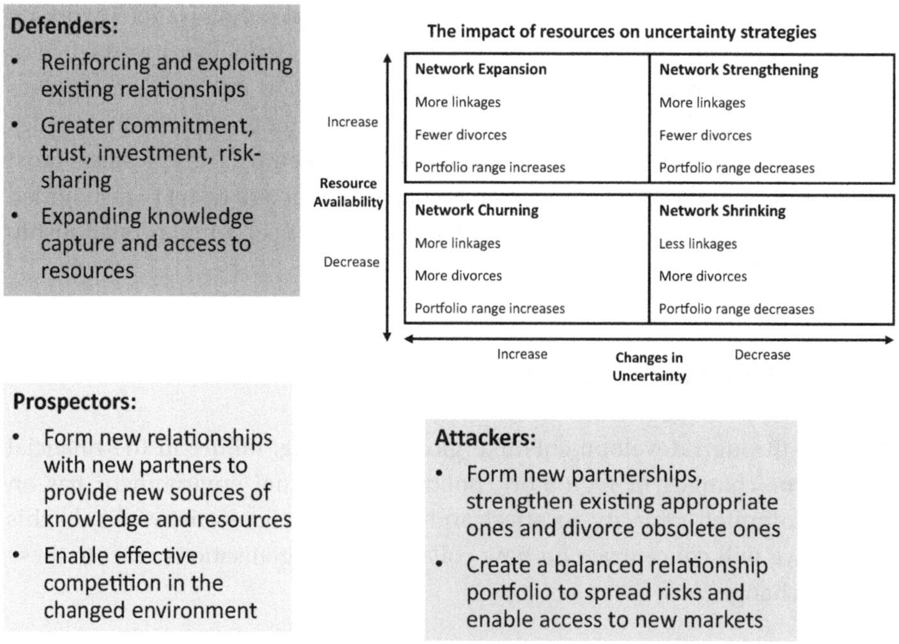

Defenders:

- Reinforcing and exploiting existing relationships
- Greater commitment, trust, investment, risk-sharing
- Expanding knowledge capture and access to resources

The impact of resources on uncertainty strategies

	Increase ← Resource Availability → Decrease	Network Expansion	Network Strengthening
		More linkages	More linkages
		Fewer divorces	Fewer divorces
		Portfolio range increases	Portfolio range decreases
		Network Churning	Network Shrinking
		More linkages	Less linkages
		More divorces	More divorces
		Portfolio range increases	Portfolio range decreases

Increase ← Changes in Uncertainty → Decrease

Prospectors:

- Form new relationships with new partners to provide new sources of knowledge and resources
- Enable effective competition in the changed environment

Attackers:

- Form new partnerships, strengthen existing appropriate ones and divorce obsolete ones
- Create a balanced relationship portfolio to spread risks and enable access to new markets

Figure 2.2   Uncertainty strategies in relationship networks

In the wider market, uncertainty is likely to affect whole sectors, and as well as being extremely hard to forecast, is very difficult to control. For instance, the impact of downloading music using file sharing services has the potential to destabilise the whole music industry. Other factors might include the competitive actions of rivals (cost cutting by budget airlines and supermarkets), demand variability (when horse meat was found to have contaminated food products in the EU) and input costs variability (such as substantial oil price increases or shortages of premium coffee supplies).

Firms use a variety of strategies to deal with uncertainty. Some examples are shown in Figure 2.2.

We have chosen to describe three particular approaches as follows.

DEFENDERS

Those 'defender' firms that are directly affected may respond by seeking greater stability through reinforcing (exploiting) existing relationships with greater commitment and trust. They hope to share risks and to expand their knowledge and access to resources. Companies in the airline industry strengthened existing relationships in response to the demand uncertainty created by the events of 9/11. Long-standing alliances, such as the Star Alliance, SkyTeam, and Oneworld, have added new partnerships to existing co-operative agreements.

PROSPECTORS

More cataclysmic changes will cause those 'prospector' firms not directly affected to attempt to reduce uncertainty by forming relationships with new network partners (exploration). They do this because new relationships are more likely to provide novel and different sources of knowledge and resources than existing relationships. Access to new critical resources will provide the means to compete in the new environment. Thus, changes in environmental uncertainty often create opportunities for entrepreneurial actions that have significant pay-offs in the future – for example, joint ventures are an opportunity to share risk, and if the risk is reduced successfully, to embark on further expansion. Deregulation in the airline industry opened up several avenues of organisational action, from pricing strategies, code sharing and the development of new hubs to the opening of new routes that were closed to certain airlines by the regulatory regime. In another example, Amazon's investment in technology, its entry into different new markets (for example, toys, electronics, kitchenware, and recently groceries) and its creation of a distribution network were facilitated by several new alliances in different sectors.

Without breaking some old relationship linkages, firms may be limited in their ability to invest additional resources in current or new alliances because low availability of resources is likely both to depress internal resources and to hamper the ability to raise resources from outside the firm. More importantly, relationship divorces may occur because existing routines between partners may be obsolete in the new environment. This is known as 'network churning'.

When the technology in the chip industry changed CISC (complex instruction set computing) to RISC (reduced instruction set computing), firms that were well entrenched in the CISC system did not form new relationships with new partners. In contrast, firms that were not part of the old CISC order forged many of the new linkages. Thus, while such a scenario involving a major shakeout and re-direction of the market players led to an increase in new alliances and partnerships, there was also considerable dissolution of existing ties.

ATTACKERS

Alternatively, rather than taking a purely reactive role, it is possible to actively pursue a relationship strategy that maximises your ability to achieve your objectives while minimising the effects of environmental uncertainty. This involves the careful selection of a portfolio of relationships that provides balanced access to the resources and capabilities required while spreading the risk of disruption from market forces.

Mère et Enfant (Palestine) treats children directly by providing medical and nutritional services in clinics in the West Bank and Gaza. As a relatively small player, it has much to gain from working with larger international NGOs, and because of its expertise in nutrition and its knowledge of the region, it has something to offer prospective partners. It has an explicit strategy of collaboration with a variety of organisations using a deliberate portfolio of high-, medium- and low-activity/profile organisations with the intention of enhancing its ability to raise funds and deliver services. Inter-organisational collaboration can therefore be a way for small, less powerful organisations to initiate changes in their fields of activity.

Figure 2.2 illustrates a number of uncertainty strategies that organisations can adopt, how they respond to events in the environment, and how the availability of resources can affect those decisions.

Organisations usually face the internal and external uncertainties of their environment in a rational and realistic way. Few are so detached from others that they can declare they do not need to take them into consideration in their strategies. The lesson is therefore to widen your strategic thinking to encompass the networks that you are part of. Some guiding principles on how to use your networks to leverage your competitive position (or how to ride the waves) are summarised as follows:

- Use network relationships as a strategic tool to minimise risks and maximise opportunities.

- Build and maintain a flexible, innovative structure.

- Use the strength of collaborative relationships to create a high-performing team that is sensitive to all the environmental developments and is adaptable.

- Ensure that the network continuously represents the best possible balance of resources and capabilities to meet its current, anticipated and potential objectives.

- Seek out organisations which will add value by joining your network.

- Divesting the network of organisations that no longer add value or are unable to adapt is essential.

Network Complexity Factors

So far, we have concentrated on the external factors that affect our ability to manage complex collaborative relationships. We turn now to the network perspective. Complex adaptive systems are a dominant feature of organisation networks. These are groups of firms and organisations which work together to manufacture and distribute products, to deliver projects and to provide services.

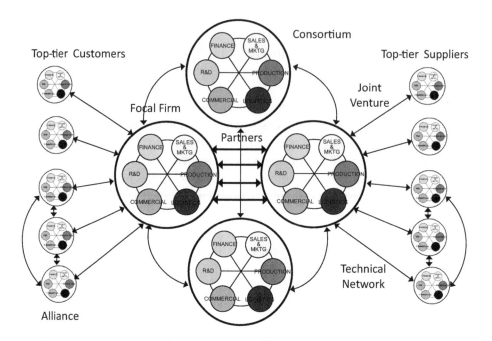

Figure 2.3   The complexity of relationship networks

STRUCTURAL DIFFERENTIATION

Figure 2.3 illustrates the fact that complexity is a function of structural differentiation. This includes the number of tiers (vertical complexity), the number of suppliers per tier (horizontal complexity), the geographical distance between firms (spatial complexity) and intangibles such as the level of coupling between firms, as indicated by the closeness of working relationships. On the latter point, it is often thought that close collaborative relationships will always be easier to manage and give rise to less complexity than those that are at arm's length. This, of course, is a fallacy. Your relationship with your local supermarket is far easier to deal with than that with a 16-year-old son or daughter! When the relationship works smoothly, the coupling may reduce complexity, but when the relationship does not work well, the fact that the two entities are closely coupled together will certainly increase the complexity.

DEGREE OF FORMALISATION

Networks will include a varying degree of formalisation. This is the extent to which they are controlled by policies, rules and procedures that prescribe the rights and obligations of the partner companies. Often the degree of formalisation will depend on the existence of a focal company at the centre of all partnering suppliers in the network. It will co-ordinate and control network activities. The key advantages of centralisation are orderliness and economies of scale.

Toyota's top-tier supplier association, Kyoryoku Kai, helps to standardise quality control procedures, diffuses Toyota's best practices and supports its long-term development. However, it may not want its suppliers to exchange information regarding bidding prices or their experience with the focal company regarding price policy. Co-operative supplier–supplier relationships can often stray into collusion, so inter-relationships in the supply base present another dimension of complexity for focal companies to manage.

The conditions that govern transactions between businesses are usually recorded in a contract. The economist and recent Nobel Prize winner Oliver Williamson recognised over 30 years ago that traditional contracts were not adequate when flexibility was required in the face of uncertainty (for example, where new products or markets were being developed), and that they increased complexity (for example, where several partners were involved). Under these circumstances, relational contracting was devised to provide a looser form of framework in which collaborative relationships could achieve their aims while still safeguarding their respective interests. Inevitably, trust came to play a more prominent role in reducing the risk of failure to perform rather than the traditional sanctions, such as penalty clauses. As a key element of this approach, contracts cover much longer periods in order to engender long-term behaviours such as learning and adaptation and to bring increased stability to the relationship. Prices and other specifications are re-negotiated regularly, but take into consideration the evolving relationship and its place in the market.

With the increased inherent complexity of today's products and services and the need to involve networks of specialised firms in their supply chains, relational governance has taken on even greater importance, which has necessarily led to the development of completely different management structures. In some networks, managers work together as if in a club with informal rules and standards of behaviour. When working closely together, it is relatively easy to see whether partners are not pulling their weight or are acting in their own interests at the expense of the team. These groups then rely on shame and guilt to dissuade members from acting opportunistically (self-interest with guile) – in effect, using a social network to manage a business network.

SEMATECH (Semiconductor Manufacturing Technology) was a consortium formed in 1987 by 14 major US semiconductor manufacturers to improve the industry infrastructure (especially the supply base of equipment and material), to improve manufacturing processes and to improve the management of factories. The individual companies were usually highly competitive, and it was realised that a traditional commercial agreement would not work. The payoffs of non-co-operation were reduced by imposing physical and psychological barriers to 'defection' and by establishing appropriate organisation structures to promote open and visible activities. The incentives to co-operate were thus greater than those to cheat.

The organisation is still in existence, and includes some of the world's major IT companies, such as IBM, Intel, NEC and Samsung.

CENTRALISATION AND DECENTRALISATION

Whether or not there is an obvious focal company in the alliance (such as in some research consortia), there will also be varying degrees of centralisation and decentralisation depending on the functions carried out and the necessity for innovation. The key advantages of decentralisation are responsiveness to local changes and an environment that is more conducive to creative ideas. This is especially noticeable for those firms located closest to customers, which will be particularly sensitive to changes in demand. The degree of innovation by suppliers is directly proportional to the amount of autonomy they have to work with customers and the different cultures and areas of technical expertise that they possess. If the function of the network is limited to the delivery of highly standardised products, then a rigid organisation framework and governance structure is likely to be appropriate. This is perhaps only a step away from being absorbed into a customer's own organisation, and is very inflexible. Moreover, it is unlikely to generate long-term partnership attitudes and benefits. On the other hand, in an outsourcing situation where network partners are expected to find creative solutions within ever-improving cost structures, informal framework contracting including profit sharing incentives is more likely to engender the co-operative behaviours that will achieve success. Honda appears to have a paternalistic formula that successfully combines both formal and informal approaches: 'Honda, often, especially at the beginning of a new product line, makes things vague on what the expectations are in terms of quality. For instance, they do not spell out the exact level of drag of a hinge as it closes and opens' (Choi and Hong 2002).

A manager at Honda explained that this initial vagueness actually helps them 'push new standards or increased quality level' during the process of working together. In the end, the supplier's overall assessment is that:

> 'Honda is usually very clear what they expect of [us]', which means that Honda has implicit yet clearly understood norms guiding its relationship with the suppliers. With all its suppliers in long-term relationships, Honda gets involved in ensuring their long-term viability. It reviews the supplier's sales, overall financial situation, annual business plans, technology development, and investment plans. According to a Honda manager, 'we watch them closely and they watch us closely, and together we come up with the best plan'.
>
> (Choi and Hong 2002)

INTERRELATIONSHIPS

Within a complex adaptive system of business-to-business relationships, everything is interrelated. Managers' decisions, such as supplier selection, shifting priorities (allocation of resources) or procedural modifications, may impact not only internal aspects such as capacity, service level or inventory, but also system factors like network efficiency, flexibility and operating redundancy. Organisations' capacity and ability to deliver service levels will often operate within very narrow confines. Hence, deciding to increase one or the other will require extensive effort and co-operation.

Honda adapted to the changing automotive sector environment by leveraging the existing experience and capabilities of its supply chain partners to develop and manufacture new products – in essence, becoming a complex adaptive system. It used its Accord and Civic platforms as the basis of several new sport utility vehicles, and as a result gained significant market share in that segment even though it was originally slow to enter the four-wheel-drive market.

NETWORK TOPOLOGY

The topology of the network also has a bearing on the ease with which changes can be implemented. Long path lengths with built-in redundancy lead to increased co-ordination problems as well as more obvious supply chain factors such as more inventory and longer times to serve. Further complexity is added when power nodes exist over clusters of organisations and which require political skills to persuade boundary-spanners to support a change in direction. Finally, the emergent/self-organising ability of a network of relationships has the ability to generate flexibility, dynamism and innovation, but it can also generate unintended outcomes.

In 1996, the US Congress passed the Healthcare Insurance Portability and Accountability Act (HIPAA), which mandated adoption of a set of regulations relating to standards and requirements for the electronic submission of health information. A key aim was to eliminate the wide variety of reporting requirements set by the multitude of healthcare providers and insurance payers. It was hoped the Act would eliminate the intermediary clearing houses which converted the diverse forms from one structure to another. HIPAA completely ignored the fact that most local providers did not have the resources to implement the changes. Facing a significant danger to their livelihood, clearing houses stepped in to provide a HIPAA-compliant information service for the healthcare providers and payers. Both gladly accepted this service, thus, instead of eliminating the clearing houses, strengthening the position of intermediaries in the supply chain.

The oil that greases the wheels of collaboration is communication. Communication broadly takes place in three functional areas: Process Control, Policy-making and Knowledge Transfer. It needs to be transparent, open, honest and frequent. It is not just governed by the need to fulfil the contract. The deeper the collaborative enterprise, the more complexity it entails, and hence the more crucial is the role of communications. Lack of effective communication is often said to be the reason for sub-optimal and failed partnerships. Without good communications, continuous improvement will always fall short of its objectives because complacency will set in.

NETWORK SIZE AND CO-ORDINATION

The larger the network and the greater the range and diversity of products, the greater will be the co-ordination difficulties. These result in increased inventory costs because of longer lead times and increased difficulties in accurate forecasting because of the numerous stages in the process. Many firms have introduced sophisticated IT systems to cascade point of sale information back down the supply chain and to choreograph the flows of parts between suppliers, manufacturers and customers. Many marketing channels are highly dependent on the flow of product information in one direction and sales/ order processing in the other. These systems require relationships to develop between the chain links to handle the exceptions that will invariably occur in dynamic and unpredictable situations. Often the driver for change may be regulatory. For instance, in the EU, concern over the environmental impact of goods vehicles has stimulated co-operation between disparate haulage companies to develop systems to enable them to maximise their capacity by minimising empty running on return journeys. However, as with safety-critical systems such as the interactions between departments that manage aircraft carrier flight deck operations or a hospital accident and emergency unit, making changes to complex systems is very much a matter of altering the embedded information flows; this is not at all easy to do. Successful 'Communication Complexity Masters' will balance their organisations' abilities with the market's needs by forecasting for capacity and executing for demand. In this way, they will succeed most of the time, only being caught out by exceptional demand peaks.

JOINT POLICIES: GETTING ORGANISATIONS TO AGREE

Discussions about policy within collaborative networks are essential to ensure all the players are committed to the same objectives and to ensure that mental models are logically consistent and rational and internal contradictions are eliminated. This is especially crucial in collaborative strategic processes, such as value specification, innovation, strategy development and performance improvement. However, forces of fragmentation such as geographic distance, different roles and involvement in different industries will need to be overcome in order to achieve the necessary collective decisions and actions. Effective collective policy-making activates informed decision-making to deal with uncertainty by integrating knowledge from all available sources (such as business intelligence, distributed intelligence and human intelligence) in a network. It is also useful in creating trusting power relationships where expectations are managed openly as well as providing an efficient co-ordination mechanism.

Organisation and Network Learning

Many organisations' prime reason for joining a consortium or alliance is to gain access to information and knowledge they do not currently have. This may be technical and concerned with manufacturing, or more strategic about operating in unfamiliar markets or access to other, more senior firms in a market sector. Network members usually assume that passing on their knowledge to other partners will benefit the alliance as a whole. However, some firms occupying strong nodal positions may act selfishly by creating and fostering information bottlenecks in order to gain for themselves the maximum knowledge value from the network. Sometimes this situation is overt, but often it is not and is not fully recognised until some event triggers resistance from the bottleneck company. Sometimes companies believe that IT provides a structured environment for collaborative network process management and also for taming the social complexity that surrounds communication, problem-solving and knowledge management. However, its very inflexibility can be a problem when seeking to implement change.

> A Greek manufacturer makes stainless steel industrial equipment for the food and alcoholic beverages industries and has many suppliers of technical equipment. Its downstream supply network includes a distribution centre/warehouse, four regional distributors, retailers all over Greece, and agents/resellers in five nearby countries. In order to make better sense of this complexity, the company introduced an Internet-based IT system to manage production, logistics, sales and order processing, and management information and communications. Implementation was not smooth, and adoption was slow.

In such situations, the leading role of the focal company is to make clear to its suppliers and customers that the software tool is just an instrument for facilitating the lean management process. It does not guarantee lean performance, and it is really up to the organisations involved to devise the appropriate means and processes for achieving it.

The Management Response

We have painted a picture of the challenges presented by the increased complexity that comes into play when working collaboratively with other organisations. At the end of the day, the manager's objectives remain relatively simple:

- How do you cut costs without reducing customer service?

- How do you manage complex relationships?

- What systematic management arrangements do you have in place?

- How do you understand performance issues?

- What criteria do you use: bottom line, effectiveness or potential?

- How do you strengthen key relationships?

- How do you manage relationships for long-term profit/value for money?

- How do you do this with minimal effort and maximum effectiveness?

Unfortunately, many organisations will turn to tried and tested management tools such as management plans, project plans, financial statements, quality plans, contract management and balanced scorecards. Conventional wisdom suggests that organisations should focus on their best customers in order to obtain long-term sustained revenues from them (approaches known as key account management, customer relationship management and other similar terms). Customers, on the other hand, will concentrate on building relationships with their most important suppliers in order to secure continuity of service and assured standards of products and services (supplier relationship management). They then wonder why their alliances and partnerships are not working as well as expected. They do not realise that traditional methods have insufficient scope, are backward-looking, fail to measure relationship performance, and most importantly, as self-centred strategies, they never meet in the middle to provide a joint focus. Because firefighting and poor teamwork tend to be the norm, the resultant performance will always be sub-optimal and will undermine efforts to undertake the essential changes that ensure firms will adapt and thrive.

In response, we provide the following summary of network management lessons:

- Knock-on effects and unintended consequences (good and bad) make planning difficult.

- Gatekeepers are never secure.

- Improve communications and you will improve performance.

- Dedicated boundary-spanning roles will resolve compatibility issues.

- Power positions tend to even out as the network gains balance and stability.

- 'Bad behaviours' can be minimised by social effects.

- Internal (network) competitive strategies are likely to backfire unexpectedly.

- The network has the capability to provide a strong, effective presence in the market, but internal complexity needs to be managed.

- 'The team is only as strong as its weakest member.'

- Continuous contingency planning will minimise external risks.

Conclusions

Collaborative network relationships set out to achieve a number of objectives while they adapt and survive. Firstly, they aim to minimise the costs incurred at the relational interface (frictional) between the partner companies where co-ordination, planning and problem-solving take place. Next, they devote effort to the creation of processes that are responsive to changing requirements while minimising disruption to the smooth, timely flow of procured goods and services from suppliers to customers. Tapping into suppliers' creativity for product and process improvements is important in most collaborative networks, and as mentioned above, requires just the right balance between formality and informality. Lastly, high complexity leads to high transaction costs and high supply risks. A reduction in complexity (for example, reducing supplier numbers) may lead to lower transaction costs and increased supplier responsiveness, but it may also reduce the levels of skills and other resources in the network. It will certainly increase management costs, because greater informality requires more frequent in-depth communication, with all the social complexity that brings. Nevertheless, in the longer term it will result in a more stable and survivable network.

Whether you are operating in marketing channels, supply chains, networks, alliances, partnerships, joint ventures or consortia, collaborative success rests upon the combination of two factors. First, organisations must use their networks, building, changing and adapting them as part of their business strategy. Secondly, they must implement enterprise relationship management in order to co-ordinate all the business activities that are essential to the success of their joint/multi-party endeavours. (We will cover this in detail in later chapters.) In the face of all this complexity, uncertainty and apparent chaos, which seem to be the norms in today's competitive environment, effective relationship management is by far the most critical success factor.

Chapter 3
The Right Culture for Collaboration

Culture eats strategy for breakfast.
(Attributed to management guru Peter Drucker[1])

Introduction

In this book we describe many things that can get in the way of effective and productive collaboration. Similarly, we discuss the many positive steps and behaviours that can be adopted that will even the odds in favour of the organisation for greater collaborative success.

However, all of these factors need to be understood in the context of the working environment. The working environment or organisational culture consists of the prevailing conditions under which we are working with others in our own organisation as well as externally.

Perhaps unsurprisingly, culture clashes are among the main reasons why alliances fail. Culture is important because it defines the lens through which problems are recognised and described. It also defines the way in which solutions are developed, formulated and actioned. As such, where there are opposing paradigms in the way business is understood and carried out, then the likelihood for partnering failure is increased. Nevertheless, these alternative culture perspectives may appear to be highly problematic, but they are rarely insurmountable barriers. Culture clashes that are disruptive tend to be brought about by the parties involved being unwilling to adapt or insensitive to the cultural practices of others. As such, an appreciation of the cultural elements that a firm may experience represents one step forward in understanding and a step closer to partnering success.

---

1   'Peter Drucker', *Reply-mc*: www.reply-mc.com/people/peter-drucker (accessed 6 September 2014).

The Importance of Culture

The way in which we are brought up, the influence of our parents and of the schools we attend and the society we inhabit affect our behaviours and our outlook on life.

All of us have values of some kind. Some are values that we can articulate clearly, such as a religious or a political persuasion; others can be less obvious to ourselves but plain to see for others. Values are beliefs that endure over an extended period that certain ways of acting or thinking are preferable to other sets of behaviours. These values are a result of many different factors and influences, from our parents, from our schools and from the environment in which we grow up. These values combine with rituals and practices, the things we do because we think they are the right things to be done. Sometimes these rituals and practices have very little real substance, whereas at other times they can be critical to our safety and well-being. Typically, we will then look around for individuals, real or fictional, who epitomise and excel in performing these rituals or demonstrating these values. These individuals then become our heroes and heroines. These values, rituals and practices combine with our identification and nomination of heroes to form our culture.

Figure 3.1   The challenge of cultural confusion

We can talk about culture in the sense of a geographic or political culture, and say that the culture of France is different from the culture in Brazil, meaning that the underlying values, heroes and rituals in France are different from those we would recognise in Brazil. Note that we are talking about cultures being different, not better than one another.

However, geopolitical culture is not the only type of culture that can influence us. While we might live within a broad culture of a country or society, we also belong to other types of cultural groups – for example, religious or political organisations. In these cultural sub-groups, we might see that the values, rituals and heroes are specific to that group of people as well as being different or distinguishable from the broader cultural group. All of this creates a managerial challenge to work collaboratively within these overlapping cultures (see Figure 3.1).

It almost goes without saying that the first and most obvious step in developing successful collaboration with a partner is the selection of the right partner. Academic theory on partner selection in collaboration between firms remains generally weak. On the one side, there is transaction cost theory, which suggests that firms choose allies by conducting a comparative assessment of the costs involved in the activity. Alternatively, the resource-based view examines the assets and resources that represent the basis for the partnership, and maintains that firms should conduct a comparative assessment of potential partners' resources and subsequently choose the strongest. However, both of these streams seem deficient. The resource-based theory aims to address which assets should be brought together, whereas transaction cost theory informs us about how these assets should be brought together. As such, we are left trying to make two halves a whole, and with a view that a more consolidated approach is probably required to make these considerations relevant for managers in particular environments.

Management texts and guidance do nevertheless exist which draw heavily on best practices from purchasing arrangements and contracting. This suggests that partner selection is typically based on a number of critical considerations: which firms are available to choose from, whether the potential partner(s) can deliver what the firm is looking for, the capacity and competencies of the firm, whether it can do it at the right price and cost, and whether the partner can ensure the requisite service levels are delivered. In this sense, partner selection takes on the characteristics of many similar make or buy, or sourcing or agency recruitment projects. Many of the factors that are examined will be quantitative, demographic and predominantly financial in their nature. If applied correctly, these will inform the decision-making process and the 'right' partner will be selected according to the chosen criteria.

Nevertheless, this approach seems a bit dated and moribund. An alternative perspective can be considered if one objective of collaborating is the contribution it can make to organisational change and creative or innovative processes and practices. In this sense, the criteria are expanded beyond the immediate economic or commercial rationale to consider whether the prospective partner is likely to be an effective collaborator, whether it represents an organisation with which the host firm could work, and whether and how it will enable the strategic logic(s) of the relationship to be attained and delivered. As such, this perspective shifts the focus from the short term and immediate to a different horizon, which is less clear-cut but potentially offers greater rewards.

Collaborative partnerships typically fail for one or a combination of three reasons:

1.   The investments made in the partnership may not be leveraged, which leads to underperformance and inefficiencies.

2.   The partners may be unable to learn from the relationship, which influences their ability to leverage investments and capture value.

3.   The partnership may be managed ineffectively with poor or unsympathetic governance mechanisms in place, which negates value capture and learning.

These three factors are influenced by the manner in which the firms involved operate and their working practices both internally and externally. As a consequence, the selection of the 'right' partner also needs to consider the cultural foundation of the firms involved:

•   the national culture;

•   the corporate culture;

•   the partnering culture.

NATIONAL OR GEOPOLITICAL CULTURE

As discussed above, we all have values. These values combine with a person's or a group's heroes, rituals and practices to form a culture. Heroes are persons, alive or dead, real or imaginary, whose characteristics are highly prized and represent models for behaviour. Rituals are common or collective actions that are technically unnecessary in achieving an end result, but that represent to the group an end in themselves. These are all buried – or, according to Hofstede (2001): 'subsumed under the term practices. As such, they are visible to an outside observer; their cultural meanings however, are invisible and lie precisely and only in the ways that these practices are interpreted by insiders.'

Therefore, national culture, on the one hand, is composed of multiple, complex elements, but on the other can be thought of as simply what distinguishes one group of people from another. Hofstede's framework is generally considered the most influential, and derived and defined through research dimensions of cultural variation (see Table 3.1). He initially identified four dimensions of national culture; the fifth dimension, long-term orientation, was added after the initial IBM-based studies. High scores for long-term orientation are less apparent in Western European countries than the significantly higher scores found among the 'tiger economies' of Asia and the Pacific Rim.

Table 3.1   Hofstede's dimensions of culture

Cultural dimension	Definition
Power distance	Social inequality. The extent to which less powerful members of an organisation and institution accept and expect that power is equally distributed.
Uncertainty avoidance	Society's attempt to deal with the uncertainty inherent in economic and social processes. The extent to which a culture programmes its members to feel uncomfortable or comfortable in situations that are new, different or unknown.
Individualism	The relationship between the individual and the group. Individualism compared to collectivism, is the degree to which individuals are supposed to look after themselves or remain integrated into groups, usually families.
Masculinity	Social implications of gender. Masculinity contrasted with femininity refers to the distribution of emotional roles between the genders that is 'toughness' versus tenderness.
Long-term orientation	The extent to which a culture programmes its people to accept deferred gratification of their material, social and emotional needs.

Source: Adapted from Hofstede (2001).

Hofstede's research is now fifty years old, and although it is generally acknowledged that culture changes slowly, the last two decades of the twenty-first century saw the significant trend of global business characterised by international and immediate communication through the Internet and telephony technology. Nevertheless, there remains evidence that cultural values are stable over time and that the outward signs of cultural convergence – for example, beverages (Coca-Cola Enterprises Inc; NYSE:CCE), fast food (McDonald's Corp: NYSE:MCD) and clothing (Levi Strauss & Co.) – are not symptomatic of changes in cultural values, even in transitioning states such as China.

These geopolitical cultural perspectives will typically influence the cognitive blueprint of how partners interpret the world around them. As such, at a theoretical level, it is possible to consider these cross-cultural differences as leading to additional transaction costs and complexity on the one hand, or on the other, creating value through the cross-fertilisation of a unique bundle of assets.

Cross-cultural alliances can lead to operational managers either becoming frustrated at the lack of success for tried and tested formulas or becoming sensitive to the different perspectives and ideologies of their partners and adapting accordingly. For instance, in Sino-foreign alliances and partnerships, it is important to adjust Western-based training programmes to the context of China, to recognise the novelty of human resources management practices and to understand the sustained importance of *guanxi* ('relationships'). Such empathy and understanding or cultural sensitivity, driven by a motivation for the partnership to succeed, will pave the way for collaborative performance. An awareness of these potential upsides and downsides of cross-cultural collaboration is a first step to effective management and possible acculturation or acclimatisation (understanding and being empathetic to cultural differences) or assimilation (adopting the values of the other culture).[2]

CORPORATE CULTURE

We can think about the culture of an organisation or a company. For instance, if you chose an iconic company such as Hewlett-Packard (HP), it is clear that it has its own culture. The geopolitical culture of a company enwraps and in some instances enables the organisational culture that is specific to the individual company.

---

2   Acculturation is the exchange of cultural features that results when groups of individuals from different cultures come into continuous firsthand contact; the original cultural patterns of either or both groups may be altered.

As such, it is easy to recognise that HP is an American company; more specifically, it is a technology-based company that has grown up in California and is at the heart of Silicon Valley. The organisational culture or corporate ethos that its founders cultivated can be seen as critical to the development of HP, becoming embedded in the 'HP Way' and seen as a competitive advantage for the firm.

When members of a company come together, they bring with them a diverse range of backgrounds, experiences and values (personal as well as geopolitical in nature). As these individuals work together, these factors will manifest themselves in many different ways, but gradually a set of norms or standards will arise which provides a framework for existing and new employees to work within. These standards become the template or benchmark for the way that things happen or get done or are perceived. Over time, we can think of this phenomenon leading onto the emergence of a more or less complex corporate or organisational culture.

Organisational culture can be described as 'the way that things happen or get done around here'. This means that it is possible to think of corporate culture as being made up of a number of elements:

- **key business processes** – how decisions are made; how information is valued, collected and processed; how leaders and staff communicate between one another and with their suppliers and customers; how work is shared and carried out;

- **tangible assets** – the people, facilities, land, resources and knowledge which shape the way processes are operated and a firm's culture;

- **formal arrangements** – the underlying mechanisms for control and command, or motivation (rewards and recognition) and governance;

- **the dominant coalition** – the goals, ambitions and strategies as well as the leadership style(s) of senior management will influence a firm's culture;

- **social systems** – the people (their personalities, status, education and socioeconomic backgrounds) and the way they interact can become embedded in an organisation;

- **technology** – the systems and technology the organisation has available to it and the manner in which it chooses to operate its investment management;

- **the external environment** – the geopolitical as well as political and economic factors operating outside the boundaries of the firm will influence the values and processes of the organisation.

Each of these seven factors plays an important role in the formation of a firm's culture. While many of these elements are material, it is not possible to go into a company, say as a new starter, and receive training or data sheets on the culture. Culture itself; it is not tangible, and can be thought of as the organisational climate, 'the feeling in the air' that you get from walking around, the perceptions of values and their interpretation by employees as well as suppliers and partners.

There is a wealth of academic literature describing corporate and organisational culture, and its associated linkages to employee satisfaction, behaviour and customers. One of the more popular streams of thought came from Charles Handy, whose work is considered to have pioneered the exploration and understanding of organisational culture and gave substance to a sometimes nebulous and complicated subject. Handy (1985) considered four types of organisational or corporate culture – power, role, task and people:

- **Power:**
  - centralisation of power;
  - emphasis on individual rather than team or committee decision-making;
  - little bureaucracy or rules and procedures;
  - fundamentally autocratic and antagonised by challenges;
  - can move quickly when threatened or faced with an opportunity;
  - little formal communication;
  - knowledge is imbued rather than managed.

- **Role:**
  - bureaucratic – its strength lies in defined functions and specialisms;
  - formality of procedures, rules, policies and guidelines;
  - job descriptions are more important that the individuals who actually perform them;

- clearly defined requirements and boundaries of authorities exist for each position;
- knowledge is compartmentalised.

- **Task:**
  - job- or project-orientated;
  - emphasis is placed on team commitment and enthusiasm;
  - influence and power are based on knowledge and skills;
  - high levels of autonomy and flexibility;
  - knowledge is power.

- **People:**
  - the individual is the focal point;
  - equality and egalitarianism are important and emphasised;
  - the growth and development of the individuals involved is paramount;
  - typical in professional, academic or research or other knowledge-based organisations;
  - management of knowledge is the lifeblood of the organisation.

An alternative but potentially overlapping perspective on corporate cultures was developed by British academics Goffee and Jones (2006), who presented a matrix that looked at organisational cultures along two dimensions (see Figure 3.2).

One axis is sociability, which is the amount of genuine friendliness among members of the organisation. In highly sociable corporate cultures, colleagues are more like friends and spend as much time interacting outside work as during it. They openly share ideas and opinions, and they exchange views on an informal and relaxed basis. Sociability comes from mutual esteem and concern for one's colleagues. The main driving forces in decisions are emotion and social concern.

The second axis is solidarity, which considers the extent to which members of the group share common objectives and aims, regardless of personal ties. A high sense of solidarity can exist in the absence of close working relationships. Solidarity is the degree to which people think together in the same ways, sharing tasks and mutual interests. The main driving force in decisions is logic.

High sociability is associated with high motivation, creativity and the freedom to think outside of the box. However, it can also be a reason why poor or ineffective working practices are tolerated for fear of upsetting friends.

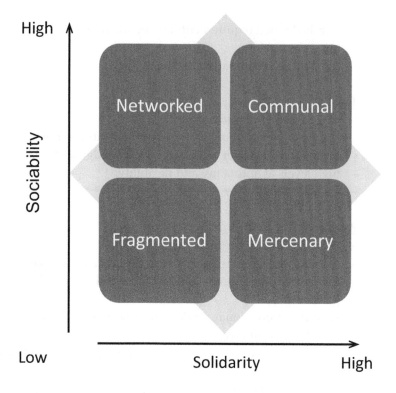

Figure 3.2   Organisational cultural matrix
Source: Adapted from Goffee and Jones (2006).

High sociability is people-based, whereas low sociability has a greater task focus. Positive sociability involves people helping one another to succeed. Negative sociability is covering up for other people and tolerating poor performance in the name of friendship or saving face. High solidarity ensures a strong and co-ordinated response to challenges and the achievement of objectives, but it also leads to high levels of conflict as teams and individuals fragment to solve problems independently. Positive solidarity gets the job done efficiently and effectively, while negative solidarity means that group members do not care for other people and can lead to high levels of internal conflict or inefficient self-interest

These two dimensions enable the characterisation of four types of culture:

- **Networked** – low solidarity and high sociability. This is characterised by people looking for ways to get around any management structures. The network culture is friendly, but work tasks are not particularly interdependent – individual, but friendly.

- **Communal** – high solidarity and high sociability. Employees possess a high, sometimes exaggerated, consciousness of organisational identity and membership. It is not unusual for people to link their self-identity with corporate identity. According to Goffee and Jones (2006), some employees at Nike have their company's trademark symbol tattooed above their ankles.

- **Fragmented** – low solidarity and low sociability. The culture here is neither friendly nor interdependent – people keep themselves to themselves, both in work and personal terms. Employees of fragmented organisations exhibit a low recognition of organisational membership. They often believe that they work for themselves or they identify with occupational groups – usually professional ones.

- **Mercenary** – high solidarity and low sociability. This is not a particularly friendly environment, but people do recognise that they need each other to get the work done. There is a real desire to achieve objectives even at the expense of colleagues.

Conclusion

Drucker's adage about culture eating strategy for breakfast seems especially relevant in international inter-organisational relationships. Many firms will enter into a partnership without pausing to consider the compatibility of their working styles or cultures. The factors that influence the potential successful outcome of a partnership can be hidden in the DNA of the companies involved. It is not necessarily the case that finding a perfect match means finding firms that think, act, and work in exactly the same ways. Conversely, while opposites can attract, the conflicts and disagreements that will arise will need to be managed, and can spur confusion as much as creativity.

This chapter has suggested that firms should consider two elements that could influence joint working: socio-geopolitical culture and organisational or company culture. Sometimes this is intuitively understood, but it can at times be less obvious and require a formal review, especially where cross-cultural understandings could, and frequently do, affect the outcome. In a digitally connected world where information and communication pass freely and quickly around the globe, it is easy to dismiss the cultural differences between us. It is important that we recognise the geopolitical culture we are working in, but equally we must acknowledge the corporate and leadership styles of the firms with which we have dealings, and how these factors interrelate.

Chapter 4

Operational Implications of Culture

Introduction

In this chapter we discuss how the broader concepts of social, political and organisational culture give rise to operational practices that directly impact upon partnership management.

We begin with a quick review of partner selection, and then the process of team formation and its application to the development of network clusters. The second section of this chapter looks at the specific element of leadership styles. Our understanding of leadership has been expanded by the very interesting GLOBE study (House et al. 2000), which related leadership preferences to geographic clusters. Finally, the third section describes how these various cultural elements can form a distinct partnering culture which influences how firms and boundary personal or relationship managers approach new and existing partnerships.

Partner Selection

It is likely that the selection of a partner will be based on economic, operational or other 'tangible' reasons, yet the ability of firms to collaborate effectively is a function of the mindsets and culture they bring to the relationship. This propensity to collaborate is influenced by the geopolitical and organisational cultures within which the partners operate or from which they emanate.

Two firms from the same culture, speaking the same language and working in the same time zone, are likely to find more common ground than alliances stretched between Bangalore and New York or Kyoto and Rochester in the USA. Nevertheless, such cross-cultural relationships are not inherently doomed to failure. Indeed, while a transactional view might suggest that this type of partnering incurs more management costs, it is equally true that the alternative perspectives can provide useful benefits. For example, the relationship between Xerox and Fuji, which we discuss in detail in Appendix 1, has been long-lasting. In its time, it has enabled Xerox to learn new skills and management approaches from its partner.

Corporate or organisational cultures are more difficult to assess. The tensions that are likely to arise between an extreme example of communal culture and a mercenary one are all too obvious. However, few organisations live at the extremes, and we can anticipate shades of grey in most situations. At the same time, while it may be desirable, it is probably not within the abilities of the partnering manager or team to change either their own or their partner's culture. Thus, an initial assessment of a potential or existing partner's culture can reveal areas of potential threat or opportunity; two fragmented cultures are likely to find collaboration more difficult than two communal cultures.

Extended Team Formation

Earlier we discussed the challenges represented by environmental and network complexity as networks proliferate, recognising that partnership life cycles are not open-ended, but are finite and time-bound. This means that firms will enter and exit more partnership relationships than previously. We will discuss the various phases of a partnership later in this chapter, but in the context of the operational implications of culture, it is important to take input from other disciples and review the Tuckman (1965) model of team formation and consider its application in networks.

The first stage is known as *forming*. At this point of time this is not a team, but a collection of individuals (firms) looking for ways to build bridges and to establish areas of common ground between them. It can be said that this stage is dominated by attempts at cohesion and involvement.

The second stage is known as *storming*. This phase is characterised by conflict, both in the formation of teams of individuals and in the development of organisational clusters and networks of firms. This conflict is associated with the establishment of leadership rights, levels or types of contributions and the limits or boundaries of the group's activities.

In the *norming* phase, the group's culture begins to be formed. In this instance, culture relates to the establishment of ways of working that are acceptable to all members of the team. Roles are established and defined, and trust and commitment are in the ascendancy.

At the next stage, the partnership, or team or network focuses on *performance* and the achievement of objectives. The nature or characteristics of the team can change as more information and experience are gained through closer working. This phase can past a long or a short time. The ability of the group to adapt to changing priorities or conditions and the addition or retirement of members may have an impact both on the group's effectiveness and its longevity.

Inevitably, the group will start to disintegrate and enter the phase known as *adjourning*. The team's or cluster's demise may be caused by many different factors, but this phase is one of reflection, learning and potentially feelings of loss or sadness.

What Do We Understand by Leadership?

As we seek to understand the culture of an organisation to be in a better position to respond appropriately to different styles of working, it is also necessary to understand the leadership style that is prevalent. The leadership style adopted by the pivotal or dominant firm in a network or cluster can have a significant impact on the nature of the relationship.

Leadership is about leading a group of people or an organisation. As such, it could be said that it is all about the needs of the people and organisation, rather than those of the leader. Having said that, selfless, self-effacing leaders are not abundant, nor perhaps the most effective. Leaders come in many shapes and guises, and similarly can adopt a range of leadership approaches or styles. For many years researchers were preoccupied with the issues of control and power – the ability to dominate and exert influence simply because you can, whatever the source of the power base. However, these ideas ignored the benefits that could be achieved through non-coercive leadership styles that typically tend to have greater currency.

Daniel Goleman is an author, psychologist and science journalist who has written extensively on. *Primal Leadership* (Goleman et al. 2004) describes six different styles of leadership:

1.   **Visionary** – This style is most appropriate when an organisation needs a new direction. Its goal is to move people towards a new set of

shared dreams. According to Goleman et al. (2004): 'Visionary leaders articulate where a group is going, but not how it will get there – setting people free to innovate, experiment, take calculated risks.'

2. **Coaching** – This one-on-one style focuses on developing individuals, showing them how to improve their performance and helping to connect their goals to the goals of the organisation. Coaching works best, Goleman et al. (2004) wrote, 'with employees who show initiative and want more professional development'. But it can backfire if it is perceived as micromanaging employees and undermining their self-confidence.

3. **Affiliative** – This style emphasises the importance of teamwork, and creates harmony in a group by connecting people to each other. Goleman et al. (2004) position their approach as particularly valuable 'when trying to heighten team harmony, increase morale, improve communication or repair broken trust in an organisation'. Nevertheless, they warn against using it alone, since its emphasis on group praise can allow poor performance to go uncorrected: 'Employees may perceive that mediocrity is tolerated.'

4. **Democratic** – This style draws on people's knowledge and skills, and creates a group commitment to the resulting goals. It works best when the direction the organisation should take is unclear and the leader needs to tap the collective wisdom of the group. Consensus-building can be disastrous in times of crisis when urgent events demand quick decisions.

5. **Pace-setting** – In this style, the leader sets high standards for performance. The leader is 'obsessive about doing things better and faster, and asks the same of everyone'. Goleman et al. (2004) warn that this style should be used sparingly, as it can undercut morale and make people feel as if they are failing. His research suggests that 'more often than not, pacesetting poisons the climate'.

6. **Commanding** – This is classic model of 'military'-style leadership – probably the most frequently used, but the least often effective. Because it rarely involves praise and often employs criticism, it undercuts morale and job satisfaction. Goleman et al. (2004) argue that it is only effective in a crisis when an urgent turnaround is needed.

The 'styles' approach to leadership built on earlier theories about the personality traits of leaders and reflected the view that leadership was as much about training as it was about the identification and selection of the right individual.

The so-called 'New Leadership Approach' of the 1990s shifted the emphasis towards leaders defining a vision, a mission and the associated accompanying values. Leadership was about making sense of what was important or needed, and we saw the emergence of the transformational or visionary leader (such as David Packard and Bill Hewlett, the founders of Hewlett-Packard`) as well as the transactional or task-oriented one.

At the beginning of the twenty-first century we heard about rock star and charismatic CEOs, such as Carly Fiorina at Hewlett-Packard, whose personas were as large as the corporate brands they represented. These have now mellowed into a more studious type of management more akin to a conductor orchestrating the whole, but recognising the importance of delegation and talent management.

The GLOBE Study

The GLOBE study (House et al. 2000) and research pull together a number of the strands of culture that we have looked at previously. GLOBE's major premise (and finding) is that leader effectiveness is contextual – it is embedded in the societal and organisational norms, values and beliefs of the people being led.

The study is particularly useful, as its starting point recognises the global or international basis of business today. It recognises that US or Western European management styles are not the best fit in all situations. Indeed, even within Europe, inter-cultural differences can and do impact management effectiveness when dealing with north and south (Finland and Italy) or east and west (Switzerland and Ireland). As a first step to gauge leader effectiveness across cultures, GLOBE empirically established nine cultural dimensions that make it possible to capture the similarities and/or differences in norms, values, beliefs – and practices – among societies which build on the research carried our by earlier researchers such as Hofstede:

- **power distance** – the degree to which members of a collective expect power to be distributed equally;

- **uncertainty avoidance** – the extent to which a society, organisation, or group relies on social norms, rules and procedures to alleviate the unpredictability of future events;

- **humane orientation** – the degree to which a collective encourages and rewards individuals for being fair, altruistic, generous, caring and kind to others;

- **collectivism I (institutional)** – the degree to which organisational and societal institutional practices encourage and reward collective distribution of resources and collective action;

- **collectivism II (in-group)** – the degree to which individuals express pride, loyalty and cohesiveness in their organisations or families;

- **gender egalitarianism** – the degree to which a collective minimises gender inequality;

- **assertiveness** – the degree to which individuals are assertive, confrontational and aggressive in their relationships with others;

- **future orientation** – the extent to which individuals engage in future-oriented behaviours such as delaying gratification, planning and investing in the future;

- **performance orientation** – the degree to which a collective encourages and rewards group members for performance improvement and excellence.

This enabled the GLOBE researchers to group or cluster countries according to these cultural dimensions, such that in the Anglo group we have Canada, the USA, England, Ireland, New Zealand and Australia. Diagrammatically opposite to the Anglo cluster is the Middle Eastern group, comprising Kuwait, Turkey, Morocco and Qatar.

The team looked at 112 leadership characteristics that were able to be statistically and conceptually reduced to 21 leadership scales which resulted in six leadership styles:

- **The performance-oriented style** (called 'charismatic/value-based' by GLOBE) stresses high standards, decisiveness and innovation, seeks to inspire people around a vision, creates a passion among organisation members to perform, and does so by firmly holding on to core values.

- **The team-oriented style** instils pride, loyalty and collaboration among organisation members, and highly values team cohesiveness and a common purpose or goals.

- **The participative style** encourages input from others in decision-making and implementation, and emphasises delegation and equality.

- **The humane style** stresses compassion and generosity, and is patient, supportive and concerned with the well-being of others.

- **The autonomous style** is characterised by an independent, individualistic and self-centric approach to leadership.

- **The self-protective** (and group-protective) style emphasises procedural, status-conscious and face-saving behaviours, and focuses on the safety and security of the individual and the group.

Table 4.1 groups the country clusters according to the degree to which they prefer each of these six leader styles. Societal clusters grouped together at the higher or lower end or in the middle differ significantly from the other groups of clusters, but not from each other. There are no statistically significant differences for the team-oriented and autonomous styles across all clusters.

Partnering Culture

Very practical research by Rolf Perie (2008) looking at the partnership between airlines and airports suggests that Cultural (geopolitical and organisational) fit alongside structural and competence fit comprise the elements of *pre-alignment*. Pre-alignment is the process through which two or more organisations can begin to work together effectively. Cultural, structural and competence fit can be thought of as forming the partnering culture that encompasses the alliance, the supply chain partnership or marketing channels.

Perie (2008) provides the definitions shown in Table 4.2 of the essential components of Partnering Culture.

Table 4.1   Country clusters and leadership preferences

Performance-oriented	Team-oriented	Participative	Humane	Autonomous	Self- or group-protective
More or higher preference					
Anglo-Germanic Nordic South East Asian Latin-European Latin-American	South East Asian Confucian Latin-American East European African Latin-European	Germanic Anglo-Nordic	South East Asian Anglo African Confucian	Germanic East European Confucian Nordic South East Asian Anglo	Middle Eastern Confucian South East Asian Latin-American East European
Confucian African East European	Nordic Anglo Middle Eastern Germanic	Latin-European Latin-American African	Germanic Middle Eastern Latin-American East European	African Middle Eastern Latin-European Latin-American	African Latin-European
Middle Eastern		East European South East Asian Confucian Middle Eastern	Latin-European Nordic		Anglo Germanic Nordic
Less or lower preference					

Source: Adapted from House et al. (2000).

Table 4.2   Elements of partnering culture

Construct	Factor	Definition
Cultural fit		The degree to which potential partners are suited for collaboration based on national, corporate or organisational culture
	Geographic culture	The influence of geopolitical enforced and created value systems and experience
	Corporate culture	The internal corporate and professional values and institutional heritage that affect a partnership
Structural fit		The degree to which potential partners are suited for collaboration based on each other's objectives, organisational structure, processes and geographic dispersion
	Objectives fit	The extent to which overlapping ambitions or threats or opportunities can be satisfied through collaboration
	Structural compatibility	The compatibility of the organisational structures, processes and knowledge bases
Competence fit		The degree to which potential partners are suited for collaboration, based on proficiency and experience
	Co-operation experience	The experience of the organisation and leader in engaging successfully in similar activities
	Organisational skills	The flexibility and adaptive skills to utilise and leverage partnering investments and assets

Source: Adapted from Perie (2008).

Cultural fit comprises the influence of corporate or individual goals on the partnership, and the extent to which physical locations and assets can be exploited beneficially by the relationship.

Structural fit has two components. The first is objectives fit, which is the precursor to the development of common goals and targets, and relates to how the strategy or mission or vision of a partner is sympathetic to the broader aims of the partnership. Within this dimension, it is also important to explore the willingness or readiness for partnering. As in any change process, there needs to be a real and recognised need to partner, otherwise the subsequent activity will be stuck in the mire of complacency, fear and self-protection. Crisis or the perception of crisis can be a real spur to creative joint working.

The definition and refinement of common goals in the development of a partnership is vitally important. Many alliances tend to be entered into with a one-sided 'What's in it for me?' attitude. This often translates to a lack of attention to determining the partner's perspective on the potential benefits, and commonly a transfer of one partner's objectives to the other. So, for example, a firm looking to develop market coverage will assume that its partner has the same or similar objectives. Furthermore, there is then the assumption that the partners will measure success in the relationship in the same manner . This will invariably lead to confusion and conflict when the partnership reaches any point of tension. Clarity gained early on in the partnering life cycle regarding the benefits each player is seeking is important to avoid conflicts of interest arising later.

Structural compatibility is the second element, and considers how an organisation's resources and processes can be made available and utilised by the partner. Common standards, IT platforms and proximity can influence structural compatibility, as can access and availability of resources – for example, warehouse capacity, patents and transferability of skills or knowledge. The leveraging of what are known as transaction-specific assets (TSAs) is a key enabler in successful partnerships.

TSAs arise out of the existing infrastructure and assets, so the starting point for their development is a review of what is currently available. For example, a review of the current staffing levels on an outsourced front office helpline could determine that certain skill sets are missing or that inadequate resources are available for peak periods. This assessment of the current resource availability leads on to a discussion of what additional or incremental capacities or capabilities are needed, and in turn can open up dialogue about how the partners might jointly address these requirements. Conversely, partnerships can be several months into a contract before the physical impossibility of achieving service levels becomes apparent.

Competence fit is the degree to which partners bring with them complementary co-operation experience, management and organisational skills. It is recognised that firms that have been good at partnering in the past will typically be good at partnering in the future. The partnering experience of the organisation and the partnering skill sets and motivation of management can have a significant effect on performance. Similarly, organisations that are rigid, inflexible and resistant to change are unlikely to morph overnight into dynamic and adaptive partners. While companies that refine and adapt their internal processes through, for example, Lean Six Sigma methodologies may be better placed to respond to the needs of partnering.

The ability of an organisation to learn and acquire new skills is critical. For many organisations, partnering is a new skill that needs to be developed. It is clearly understood that dedicated alliance managers or departments are a boon to alliance performance, therefore understanding the individual strengths and experience of the prospective partners' teams is important. Critically, research by Gibbs and Humphries (2009) has suggested that it is not only the competencies of the organisation or the partner account teams that is important, but also that of senior management.

One respondent to a Gibbs and Humphries's research initiative characterised their senior management as 'fair weather friends' – keen to support the partnering initiative on day one and when things were going well, but eager to distance themselves when times got tough. Conversely, where leaders are experienced and genuinely motivated to develop the relationship, they will take time out from their agendas to manage issues and the complex demands of internal and external stakeholders.

All of these elements can and should be weighed and measured. They will set the foundation for the further development of the partnership, or provide indications of possible issues and conflicts. Many firms enter into an alliance looking solely at the commercial or operational requirements of the partnership. Perie (2008) and others have indicated that the operating culture can be a critical factor in laying a firm foundation for success, therefore a review of the national or corporate cultures, structural fit and competence fit which combine to form the partnering culture becomes an exercise in due diligence and preparation.

Conclusions

Understanding the geopolitical or organisational culture of your partners is important. Relationship managers need to be aware of all factors that will influence the performance of the partnership. While several decades old, the Tuckman (1965) model remains apposite for providing a particular insight into how networks and clusters of firms are established. The development of serial relationships, as in the case of marketing channels, necessitates that the lead or organising firm is able to seek out and then initiate relationship development quickly.

In marketing channels, it was not uncommon to find reference to the 'channel captain' – the organisation or firm around which the channel was formed.

Logically, in many instances this was the original equipment manufacturer (OEM), but over time this could shift to a distribution and logistics organisation or a solution provider or consolidator, or even an end point customer. In such instances, the leadership style of the individuals and firms involved become readily apparent.

In the IT sector in the 1980s and 1990s, Novell adopted a benevolent collaborative approach to channel management. As a small Utah-based networking software company, it was struggling to compete against the might of larger corporations such as IBM. Its strategic decision to sell through marketing intermediaries into the lucrative small and medium-sized company sector was backed up by a well-developed and mature channel management style. Novell's channel offering embraced more than just the product; it offered accreditation and certification programmes that enabled smaller channel players to enjoy high margins in a growth segment. However, Novell went further by engaging in frequent dialogue and information-sharing. It formed partner councils, established partner clubs and held well-attended annual conferences. Novell was able to create channel partner loyalty through its affiliative leadership style, utilising the skill of its partnership managers to form and normalise relationships quickly and effectively and create a well-embedded partnering culture. This loyalty from its channel partners created a competitive advantage that in turn led to a profitable market share. In later years, new management brought in different leadership styles which negated much of the partnering culture and probably spurred Novell's fall from market and industry prominence.

Chapter 5
Drivers to Success

Introduction

The three big issues that have confronted businesses over the last ten years remain fixed firmly high on the management agenda:

1. **globalisation** – the need and ability to leverage opportunities (and manage risks) on a truly international basis, enabling access to new skills, know-how, and resources (not just cost arbitrage);

2. **information technology** – enabling the adoption, internalisation and realisation of the benefits from new technologies to the advantage of the firm;

3. **innovation** – the imperative to constantly and consistently innovate and change in the context of world markets and technological progress.

As a result of these directions, we have seen rapid change in organisational structures that have looked beyond the boundaries of the firm to collaborative working with partners to provide outsourced services to the firm while allowing it to concentrate on its core competences.

Hand in glove with these newer fragmented or extended organisational forms, we have seen increasing antagonism from managers who look at their external relationships and raise concerns about the following issues:

*   **A general lack of trust** – The proliferation of alliances, outsourcing arrangements and partnerships suggests that firms are more likely to be involved in networks and clusters of relationships, as opposed to dyadic relationships. Among the cluster, it is increasingly likely that a focal firm will find not only suppliers, but also customers and competitors, with the consequence that firms may become less willing to share information.

- **The risk of talent poaching** – Organisations of all sizes are increasingly recognising that much of their future prosperity and well-being are intrinsically bound up with their talent pool. The development and retention of key personnel (management fast tracks) is very important, and the risk of losing such staff to a partner can be very real.

- **Concerns about protection and security of intellectual property as well as know-how and expertise** – Non-disclosure agreements of one type or another abound in partnerships, but a concern often raised by management is the extent to which these and other agreements actually protect a firm's intellectual property. Similarly, as collaboration improves and produces tangible benefits, firms can become concerned about how they can protect and capitalise on the development of new ways of working, process improvements and even understanding and know-how.

Firms will raise these and other concerns as reasons why they do not want to enter into collaborative relationships or as the explanation for why such partnerships fail to develop and fulfil their potential.

It is possible to identify a number of general factors that can impact a partnership's performance, but the prime cause of poor performance in collaborative business relationships is underestimation and under-appreciation of the management task:

- A general lack of commitment caused by among other things a fear of failure and a lack of control is often manifested in inadequate joint planning, investment, staffing and management structures.

- Adversarial and bureaucratic commercial practices can result in 'them and us' attitudes; selfish behaviours then compound poor communication to cause increased costs and delays and reduce trust.

- Poor joint performance measures and systems result in incompatible objectives, disjointed processes, poor quality, higher costs and poor customer service.

- In a collaborative business relationship, each party's freedom of action is necessarily reduced, and they may have feelings of uncertainty and risk because they are dependent on each other.

Table 5.1   The four Ps of collaborative change

People	Process
The correct functional resources and skills are available. Managers understand and use emotional intelligence to manage diverse teams. Change management practices are deployed.	The end-to-end processes are understood in relationship to the value chains and competencies of the organisations. All critical inputs and outputs are mapped. Non-value steps can be identified and removed. The partnership is aligned to creating joint value.
Platform	**Programme**
IM systems are supportive of collaborative working, enable sharing of information and knowledge and performance tracking. IT is used to track and monitor progress and populate process metrics, which are critical to quality.	Collaborative programmes are managed effectively to build trust and commitment between the partners. Senior managers sponsor the programmes and dedicated 'collaboration' managers engage on a daily basis with the teams.

Understanding the Management Task

There are no short cuts in the effective management task associated with partnering. Firms need to invest in the four major components of management: people, processes, platform and programme. These elements can be thought of as building a strategic framework (see Table 5.1).

It is important to stress the word 'invest' in this context. Some firms will completely fail to recognise the need for these elements, while others will pay lip service to them, and as a result fail to ensure that they receive the necessary attention or investment:

- **People** – There are three elements to this. It should go without saying that if the resources are not available, then the programme or project will struggle, or even fail. Key resources (not necessarily expensive ones) may be unavailable; financial analysts or project managers may frequently be missing or overstretched. Secondly, it is important to recognise that collaboration is a skill set: firms can alter their recruitment, training and reward systems to focus on soft skills such as communication, team motivation and co-ordination. Key managers need to be able to lead and support the change, and this is a function of their experience as well as their skills. Thirdly, most collaborative activity with a third party will have implications on people, who will respond positively or negatively depending on how the activity has been managed. Firms need to recognise and embrace change management processes in the context of partnering and inter-organisational process improvements.

- **Processes** – Collaboration is not an episodic event. It takes place over time and changes over time. Understanding the dynamics and significance of the processes central to the collaboration is a critical task. Many organisations will assume incorrectly that they understand implicitly the various process flows, inputs and outputs that are taking place between them and their partner(s). Therefore, it is important that there is fact-based knowledge and understanding of the separate and joint processes that form the purpose and aims of the endeavour – the essential 'Why are we doing this?' In this context, 'processes' encapsulate the traditional framework of joint purpose, quality-critical metrics and boundary conditions.

- **Platforms** – The focus of IT investments over the last ten to fifteen years has been on enterprise-wide systems that have connected the back offices, front offices and, through Internet portals, customers. Firms like SAP, Oracle, and IBM have enabled organisations to link their functional operations, typically starting with back office functions like accounting, under one umbrella system. The next phase of investment management's development will be to extend and to develop new solutions that enable teams to collaborate and work together across functional groups and geographies as well as organisational boundaries. In this context, platforms also extend to the ability to manage the alliance or partnership; in a fragmented and global partnership, to consider alliance or supply chain management without considering the compatibility and effectiveness of the IT platforms that facilitate this management is not viable.

- **Programme** – In this context, this refers specifically to programme or partnering management. Successful programme management is a result of focusing on those elements that make a critical difference between high-performing partnerships and failing ones, such as trust and commitment.

Relationship Management

When a firm enters into a partnering relationship or alliance of some form, the managers involved find themselves in unfamiliar territory. Partnerships and working with other firms add complexity. Managers realise that they need to understand the processes and ways of working of their new partners, and also gain a deeper appreciation of their own organisation. The difficulty of control and direction within a single entity is amplified in cross-organisational arrangements where managers find that they lack the authority and autonomy they are used to and need to operate in a context beyond their experience. The achievement of the partnership's objectives can then be further impeded by subsequent increases in misunderstandings, poor communication and limited information-sharing, which can eat into the very heart of the relationship.

Despite all these shortcomings, effective and successful partnerships can generate significant competitive advantages for firms if properly managed. This conundrum can be addressed by gaining a better understanding of the key components of partnership business.

A relationship marketing paradigm or perspective contributes to the discovery of the drivers – the factors that can be correlated to the generation of 'relational rents'. These are above-normal profits, jointly generated in a partnering relationship that could not be generated by either firm in isolation and can only be created through specialised inputs from both alliance partners working together.

It is clear that individuals and organisations can and do identify specific factors that affect relational performance in their dealings with other firms. This can be thought of as the strength or otherwise of the relationship. It is also clear that some relational performances are better than others, and that good performance is rewarded by improved relationship outcomes. This relationship premium can be tangible in terms of increased sales, lower costs or better response times and improved service levels. It can also result in faster time to market and more innovative collaborative working.

It is possible to identify six 'super-factors' and components as the building blocks of effective relationship marketing and productive partnerships, ensuring that performance targets can be achieved to the mutual satisfaction of both or all parties:

1.   trust;

2.   commitment;

3.   conflict management;

4.   collaboration;

5.   communication;

6.   value creation.

TRUST

The construct of trust has been the subject of much academic research and interpretation. We can consider trust as the extent to which a partner will live up to its promises, has the resources and skills to do so, and will use these to the benefit of both parties. Trust also encompasses the idea that a partner believes that a firm will consider its needs and requirements when setting and deploying its strategies and policies. As such, it is about honesty and integrity as much as reliability and dependency – that is, 'walking the talk'. Trust can be contrasted with the notion of power and the use of coercive practices to achieve objectives through fear and intimidation (see Table 5.2).

It is clear that when a firm can discern reliability, dependency and the successful fulfilment of expectations, then it will begin to trust its partner, and this in turn will strengthen the willingness of the parties to rely on each other, further expanding the partnership. In this way, trust fuels collaboration and encourages communication, and vice versa.

Trust is a fundamental element within any relationship, and it is unlikely that, in the absence of other factors such as contractual obligations or legal requirements, a relationship where the parties do not trust their partners will last long. It therefore follows that trust is a key factor in the longevity of a relationship. It is also important at the start of the relationship, through the development phase as well as into maturity. At the start of the relationship, where those involved have little to go on, firms will rely on the reputation and credibility of the partner to deliver on its promises.

Table 5.2   Power and trust

	The power game	The trust game
Modus operandi	Create fear	Create trust
Guiding principle	Pursue self-interest	Pursue what is fair
Negotiating strategy	Avoid dependence by playing multiple partners off against each other Retain flexibility for yourself, but lock in partners, raising their switching costs	Create interdependence by limiting the number of partners Both parties signal commitment through specialised investments which lock them in
Communication	Primarily unilateral	Bilateral
Influence	Through coercion	Through expertise
Contracts	'Closed' or formal, detailed and short-term	'Open' or informal and long-term
Conflict management	Reduce the potential for conflict by drawing up detailed contracts Resolve conflicts through the legal system	Reduce the potential for conflict by selecting partners with similar values and by increasing mutual understanding Resolve conflicts through procedures such as mediation or arbitration

Source: Adapted from Kumar (1996).

The close collaboration of small teams that work on confidence-building projects can quickly overcome any earlier lack of experience. They can establish trust as a virtuous cycle and be a catalyst for the development of trust over time, confirming or negating initial impressions . In this respect, trust is interlinked with commitment, and whether trust builds commitment or the other way around, the two support the relationship together.

While the early work on trust versus power may seem very remote, it is not too difficult to envisage the working environment that Kumar (1996) was envisaging.

COMMITMENT

Commitment can be considered the extent to which the parties involved envisage a benefit of some kind that they cannot achieve elsewhere and which they want to enjoy over time or are prepared to wait for – a deferred benefit. This benefit can take many forms. It can be know-how or access to resources or markets, or indeed the profitability of a supply chain relationship.

Commitment is frequently accompanied by a propensity to invest in a relationship in terms of funds, people or other resources. This can take the simple form of releasing staff for training on a partner's sales system, or it can be demonstrated by the construction of a warehouse co-located with a partner.

Commitment can be better understood by examining its constituent parts:

- **Continuance commitment** – Also known as 'calculative trust', this is the degree to which a firm feels a need and desire to maintain a relationship on the basis of a rational economic desires or needs. The significance of continuance commitment as a component of commitment is clear in many situations, including supply chain and marketing channels. Continuance commitment, the economic rationale, is a key driver to the longevity and continuity of the relationship and commitment.

- **Affective commitment** – This can be defined as the level of unity perceived in a channel relationship about the extent to which members want to maintain the relationship. A sense of unity is likely to be apparent when an intermediary feels that a partner shares common business interests and goals.

- **Behavioural commitment** – This is the extent to which a firm provides special help to its partners in times of need. It has proven difficult to define behavioural commitment because of the problems of understanding what behaviours actually entail commitment. Behavioural commitment is apparent when a relationship is tested, and is revealed more clearly under difficult conditions rather than business as normal.

CONFLICT MANAGEMENT

Conflict in any relationship is inevitable. In some instances it is the natural challenge of differing views and opinions that can eventually result in a new and radically better solution being arrived at. However, not all conflict is constructive, and it is important to understand the potential sources of negative or destructive conflicts that could undermine performance.

A key source of conflict arises when the aims and objectives of the parties involved are not compatible or aligned. In such instances, the rationale for the partnership comes into question as the common purpose influencing why the firms had considered working together becomes eroded.

At the outset of the relationship, the firms may have considered that there were sufficient synergy and common interest to form the basis of a successful partnership. It then becomes important to translate these high-level ambitions into clear-cut plans and objectives. These objectives are not immutable and it should be possible to change and develop them as the relationship itself changes and develops. Nevertheless, ensuring that there is common agenda with consistent metrics is important in order to manage potential areas of conflict.

Destructive conflict can arise at any point in time, and it can be gauged in terms of the severity and frequency of disagreements. Normal everyday friction occurs in any working relationship, but such issues should be managed appropriately through escalation processes so that they do not accumulate and grow into issues that could reduce the level of trust in a relationship and hence reduce commitment.

Conflict mitigation or reduction is best accomplished through the creation of trust and commitment. At the same time, where firms engage in frequent and open dialogue and information-sharing, the opportunity for disagreements to fester is significantly reduced. The adage 'it's good to talk' remains equally true in partnerships. Proactive and positive management of management conflict can effectively increase the level of trust in a partnership and commitment as well as strengthening the relationship overall.

COLLABORATION

Effective collaboration is a key driver to relationship performance outcomes. Successful collaboration leads on to more and better collaboration as experience and confidence fuel the sparks of innovation and creativity.

Collaborative activity is dependent upon efficient co-ordination and planning, which themselves require effective communication and efficient co-operative activities. Firms have different working practices, and establishing a common approach to collaboration across organisational boundaries can be difficult. A simple fallback in joint planning is the establishment of long lists of actions and activities with accompanying metrics – for example, agreeing a number of sales engagements with prospects. Typically, such detailed approaches peter out and are not successful because the essential initial validation of common aims and common purpose has not taken place, and one partner will look to drive the other to deliver. In such situations, lip service is typically paid to operational accountability. Good collaboration results from a shift away from this account management mindset to one of business management.

This means that firms should recognise that alliance and partnership managers require different skills from sales and operational managers. The development of these 'newer' business management skills is essential for effective collaboration. In those organisations that have learnt the skills and gained the know-how to work collaboratively, there are practised processes and procedures and an established structure. These ensure the sharing of best practices and the transfer of knowledge and understanding through syndicates, workshops and networks promoting partner communication, co-ordination and co-operation.

COMMUNICATION

It almost goes without saying that communication plays an important role in the successful development of any partnership. Equally clearly, most firms overestimate the extent and appropriateness of communication.

Academics such as Anderson and Narus (1991) and Davis and Spekman (2003) have explored the construct and importance of communication. Good communication is about timeliness, relevance and accuracy. Inaccurate and late information is obviously of little value, but if the information is shared with the wrong target audience, then it is equally redundant.

Information needs to be shared and socialised, and not simply cascaded. Good communication is therefore a bi-directional activity where both parties are sharing and exchanging information and know-how. As a consequence, good communication is essential for good collaboration, and is a major factor in effective joint planning.

Communication is also critical in the development of trust throughout the life cycle of the partnership. Few partnerships will progress from initial engagement to exploration and maturity without the creation of trust, and trust in itself is encouraged by effective bi-directional communication.

It is important to recall that information-sharing and communication are fundamental to the creation of knowledge, which leads on to the ability to create relational rents within partnerships. Tacit knowledge – knowledge and understanding that is embedded within an organisation in a nebulous and typically unstructured manner – is unlikely to be disclosed or shared where some level of trust has not been established. Therefore, whereas it can be argued that information and the development of trust are interactive, the progression from information-sharing to learning is most likely to come about once trust is established.

VALUE CREATION

Value creation is a dimension that stands on its own, and will be described in more detail in the next section. The key distinction to be made, however, regards the creation of value rather than simply value-add. The creation of value goes hand in hand with the ability to capture value to the organisation's profit and loss, to the interests of the shareholders or the benefits of staff or employees. Created value need not be wholly tangible; it may be knowledge or know-how or even true intellectual property in the sense of patentable innovation.

The Dynamics of Partnering Success

Putting in place the correct management infrastructure is the first step to partnering success. Understanding and acting upon the relational aspects of partnering can then be accelerated. Trust, commitment, conflict management and collaboration are the building blocks of effective relationship management. These can be synthesised into three dimensions generating partnering performance and culminate in partnering excellence that have as their consequence the extraordinary gains and benefits of successful business-to-business partnerships:

1. **Collaborative innovation** – These conditions describe the effectiveness of the relationship and enable the partnership to be innovative and to respond to opportunities. This includes co-operation as well as communication.

2. **Partnership quality** – This concerns the quality of the relationship exchange, including commitment and trust and their counterpart, conflict.

3. **Value creation** – This focuses on the efficiency of the partnership to create and capture the potential value the partnership offers.

Table 5.3   The main components of collaborative innovation

Creativity		Communication	Co-operation
Adaptability	Innovation	Quality, relevance, timeliness and openness of communication	Extent to which the partners co-operate effectively
Ability of the partners to adapt to changing conditions	Extent to which the partnership encourages innovation and high performance	The ability of the partners to communicate effectively and efficiently	Ability of the partners to develop and manage their teamwork
			Ability of the partners to develop, manage and maintain a collaborative relationship

COLLABORATIVE INNOVATION

Collaborative innovation concerns the actions that are promoted and encouraged as a consequence of satisfactory partnership activities, such as joint working and common change initiatives. It is this aspect of a good relationship that is most often thought of as a hard-working partnership. This is the engine house of success, but without coaxing and encouragement, partnerships often stall and fail to 'spark'. Collaborative innovation can be thought of as the effectiveness of the relationship as it produces tangible outcomes such as share of wallet, growth and scale/frequency of joint projects and bids. Collaborative innovation enables partnerships to achieve their fundamental aims and objectives. The components of this factor are shown in Table 5.3.

These are typical symptoms of ineffective collaborative innovation:

- Responsibilities are shirked.

- Information is not shared effectively.

- There are pockets of understanding – the 'inner circle' mentality.

- 'Intellectual snooping' – information is collected informally by a partner.

- The focus is on the product rather than the solution for the customer.

- Account managers become 'problem-solvers' or 'query managers'.

- There are a large number of transactional, low-value or frequent sales.

- Internal processes are used to manage external partners.

- There is overt reliance on the host to initiate activities and come up with ideas.

- Customers are mis-sold products.

- There is a lack of strategic selling skills, which results in product benefit being dominant in marketing and sales activities.

- Falling customer satisfaction results from poor behaviours displayed by one or both/all partners.

- Recruitment of partners is difficult.

- Dedicated partner managers have multiple accountabilities.

- Planning workshops are dominated by business reviews.

- Joint planning sessions are task/target cascades.

PARTNERSHIP QUALITY

Partnership quality is the second key driver of the overall success of a commercial or inter-organisational relationship. It forms the basis for partnership productivity. Partnership quality is not simply a passive contributor to alliances, but directly influences important factors such as the duration and longevity of the relationship itself. This super-factor is also associated with overall satisfaction, and forms a hard link between the operational performance of the business and the effective evaluation of partnership success. Partnership quality is also a strong indicator of a firm's ability to capture the value created by an effective partnership. This is to take the gains and benefits to the bottom or top line of the profit and loss or the value for money target. Table 5.4 summarises the main components of partnership quality.

Table 5.4   The main components of partnership quality

Commitment	Trust		
Partners take a long-term view of the relationship	Interdependence	Social bonding	Trust
Partners 'live' their commitment to the joint enterprise	Partners accept that they must rely on each other to deliver the joint outcomes	Encouraging a professional, concerned attitude between firm personnel	Ensuring that joint achievements are reinforced so that staff are prepared to 'go the extra mile' to ensure that success is sustained
The partners invest in assets that build and sustain the capability of the relationship	Sharing knowledge and fostering learning to allow the partners to develop their capabilities		

Typical symptoms of inadequate trust and commitment, which undermine partnership quality include the following:

- Partners reduce investment in the host's brand or service, or in the overall relationship.

- One party is seen as a minor player in a broader network of alliances, and is (often unintentionally) excluded from key events.

- Partners compete for major accounts with alternative partners.

- Partners do not make key senior or support staff available for meetings or training.

- End customer business experience is poor.

- Relationship investments are under-utilised or 'stranded'.

- New initiatives are not adopted wholeheartedly or are missed altogether.

- Relationships are typically short-lived.

- Value cannot be captured, and neither the costs nor the gains can be accounted for.

- Unrealistic objectives are set, and there is an expectation that high returns are possible in the short term.

- There is misappropriation of partners' resources, such as technology, customers and staff.

VALUE CREATION

As well as adding value, value creation is a vital reason for organisations to work together. This is the stimulus to develop something new beyond the initial reason for the partnership. The ability of firms to capture the total value – value realisation in the form of benefits to the end customers and ultimately to the firm's profitability – is the ultimate objective of a partnership or alliance. Creating value can also be associated with service quality and perceived service quality. Many managers are aware of the importance of operational excellence, and will focus much effort on understanding their relative standard of performance. However, while the operational satisfaction of a strategic partner remains important, a more critical set of factors needs to be considered that relates to the ability of the relationship itself to add, create and capture value, and furthermore, to do this consistently over time within a stable relationship.

Table 5.5   The main components of value creation

Productive synergy		Value capture	Efficiency
Conflict management	Synergy	Ensuring a joint focus on brand, product, profitability and customers	Ensuring the joint enterprise focuses on efficient customer satisfaction
Resolving problems quickly and fairly	Clear, compatible objectives	Using a balanced, adaptable commercial framework that incentivises high performance, includes equitable profits and other benefits sharing and, encourages the relationship to develop	Ensuring the contract outputs are delivered efficiently
Encouraging creative conflict	Working to joint performance targets		Ensuring that a continuous quality improvement ethos is developed and sustained
			Ensuring that performance measurement is effective and includes the joint relationship

While it is important that partners are satisfied, it has been found that operational performance satisfaction (for example, with a query management system) does not automatically lead to increases in profitability or sales or satisfied stakeholders. On the other hand, creating and capturing value can be considered as the efficiency rating of a relationship, as it influences the return on marketing investment, return on investment and value for money as well as the gross margins of the firms involved. Inevitably, therefore, value creation is the sum of all the relationship-building, sustaining and developing behaviours that take place. Thus, concentration on only a sub-set, such as financial measures, is unlikely to achieve the full potential of the combined enterprise. Table 5.5 summarises the main components of value creation.

Typical symptoms of situations where this value creation is not being performed effectively include the following:

- Recruitment and/or retention of partners is problematic.

- Intermediaries look to justify the need for higher margins to support product/service sales.

- Intermediaries cherry-pick models.

- There are overt conflict and frequent disagreements.

- There is micro-management of operational metrics.

- Tactical programmes are used as a pricing tool.

- Partners' investment in the relationship is minimal.

- Senior management involvement is minimal.

- A partner seeks ongoing funding from a host to support any activity.

Measuring Partnering Performance

Managers need to understand which levers to pull – which performance drivers are important. This is a question that causes a great deal of controversy and confusion, and in practical terms, the idea of taking positive actions to influence a business relationship is like trying to grip a piece of wet soap. Current methods of judging the value and performance of a partnership generally address the usual time, cost and quality criteria. They include scorecard approaches, quality systems, risk assessments, project plans, value chain analyses and financial tools such as balance sheets and investment appraisals. These focus on highly detailed indicators and often use historical, subjective data. Unfortunately, as many managers will bear out, these systems take a one-sided view of the partnership, and miss the key pointers to those activities and interactions between firms that drive successful, collaborative operations. As a result, managers feeling out of touch and are prone to firefighting problems that appear to come from nowhere.

THE PARTNERING BEHAVIOUR FAILURE SPIRAL

To start with, let us take a contrary scenario that reveals the tendency of people to 'shoot from the hip' when they are not sure what to do. The uncertainty of dealing with a partner can cause firms to focus primarily on their own objectives and to take advantage of any weakness in the other side to improve their position, or themselves risk being taken advantage of. Experience and knowledge limitations together with fear of the unknown will persuade managers to keep to those practices and processes with which they are most familiar – their comfort zone. This translates into a firm doing as little as possible to adapt to changing conditions, and often very little to modify its processes to accommodate the partner's world. At the same time, this makes organisations more risk-averse, and they will tend to take short-term gains rather than risk longer-term uncertainty. This creates more risk. Partners are therefore minded to reduce levels of investment in the partnership, including the exposure of their trade secrets, the deployment of expertise and training efforts. Faced with this behaviour, the partner company is minded to react in a similar way, and if managers are not careful, a culture of tit for tat will set in which inevitably saps the value generated by the joint business. In engineering terms, this is a negative feedback loop. Worse still, this situation becomes accepted as the inevitable result of management complexity and costs that are expected in business relationships. We call this the failure spiral because it shows the relationship dynamics at work when negative behaviours are considered in their worst light (see Figure 5.1).

In 2000, the UK Defence weapons systems support teams and their collaborative industrial partners had been working for three years to improve the efficiency of their collaborative relationships under a programme called Smart Acquisition. A key part of this initiative was to establish joint working within integrated project teams. These organisations ensured that the Navy, Army and Air Force front-line units' weapons and equipment (such as ships, tanks and aircraft) were properly supported with spare parts, repairs and modifications. These relationships between the UK Ministry of Defence and the world's major defence companies were strategically important because they maintained and enhanced national defence capability, and moreover, they involved a considerable expenditure of public money – nearly £12 billion in 2001.

In the past, there had been a long-held perception by the government that these relationships did not give best value for money, and that adversarial and opportunistic practices were the cause. Some high-profile failures, such as tanks and rifles that were vulnerable to sand clogging during the first Gulf War, underlined the political and public concerns about the defence equipment business. From the industry perspective, this was a hugely costly and risky business. Returns took many years to materialise and the customer did not really understand the technology, frequently changed its mind and distrusted the suppliers' profit motives, exacerbating the problems.

Figure 5.1   The Partnering Behaviour Failure Spiral

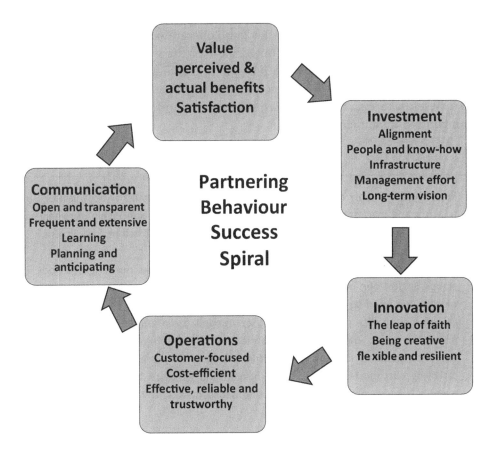

Figure 5.2   The Partnering Behaviour Success Spiral

THE PARTNERING BEHAVIOUR SUCCESS SPIRAL

Of course, there is an alternative view, because we have all heard about or experienced successful alliances. In these cases, positive interaction forces can be viewed as the self-reinforcing, positive feedback loop or success spiral shown in Figure 5.2.

In this scenario, the business case for the partnership is also strong, but the parties are openly enthusiastic about achieving their joint aims. They concentrate on getting products and their delivery right, which prompts staff to look for innovation in both the offerings and their production. The organisations feel optimistic, and invest in the relationship by adding further resources and know-how. Communication at all levels begins to develop, and the partners believe that they have backed a winner. In consequence, renewed efforts are devoted to the joint operation ... and so on. Some might consider this to be a rose-tinted view of the world, but major firms such as Coca-Cola show that it is possible to create and sustain a virtuous business relationship cycle. Moreover, it is high-performing relationships like these that are gaining above-average returns and continuously creating competitive advantage.

In the baking supply chain, farmers had created an intermediary organisation to store and market their grain. As a result, a very close relationship between the intermediary and the milling companies and the bakers had been built. The farmers gained accurate planning information and feedback to enable them to develop new strains of wheat: 'Our intermediary speaks our language and stands-up for our interests with our customers. We have a very clear idea of what we need to do, and we always do our best to do it.' The customers gained high-quality products when they needed them and at a competitive price. Moreover, important R&D carried out by the farmers ensured they could continue to develop competitive products: 'We are all committed to satisfying customers, and will move heaven and earth to be the best in the market. There is a lot of trust all around because we know that everyone is a vital link in the chain.'

These performance spirals seem to tap the key components of partnership success and failure, and allow us to derive five performance measures, as shown in Table 5.6.

Table 5.6   Relationship spiral performance measures

Failure spiral	Success spiral	Performance measure
Confinement and pressure	Value	Equality
Self-interest	Reliability	Operations
Least effort	Creativity	Innovation
Low commitment	Stability	Investment
Information economy	Communication	Communication

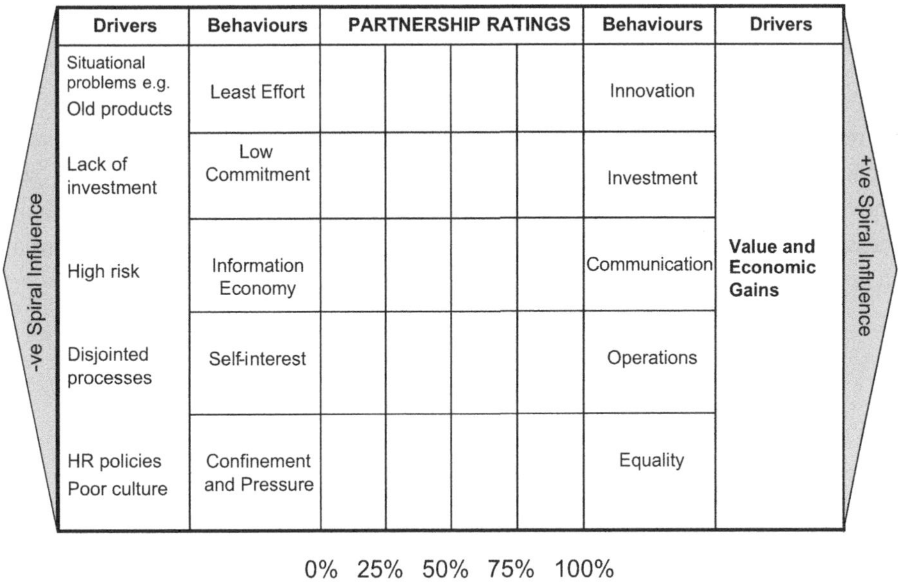
Drivers
Behaviours
PARTNERSHIP RATINGS
Behaviours
Drivers
Situational problems e.g. Old products
Least Effort
Innovation
Lack of investment
Low Commitment
Investment
High risk
Information Economy
Communication
Value and Economic Gains
Disjointed processes
Self-interest
Operations
HR policies Poor culture
Confinement and Pressure
Equality
-ve Spiral Influence
+ve Spiral Influence
0% 25% 50% 75% 100%

Figure 5.3 Partnership performance matrix

In reality, alliance managers will be aware of a spectrum of success and failure dynamics under each of these performance measures that span their commercial relationships – the tendency towards the spiral of success or the spiral of failure. Therefore, if the right questions can be devised and put to managers in each firm which is party to an alliance, some important performance metrics can be generated and plotted in the matrix shown in Figure 5.3.

It should then be possible to follow up these pointers to enable all concerned to understand the particular reasons why performance is good or not so good, and as a result of this, to mobilise support to make changes. If this measurement process is repeated periodically, we have a means of driving continuous relationship improvement and, for the first time, giving relationship managers a tool that lends some power to their elbow to support their efforts to achieve change.

Conclusions

The complexity of the task of managing partnerships effectively is now better understood than ever before. We have the advantage of seeing inter-organisational relationships through the lens of the relationship marketing paradigm.

The importance of the so-called soft factors of business relationships is now far more clearly recognised in many corporations. We recognise that organisations are composed of individuals, and that individuals do recognise and respond to relational stimuli. The importance of the strength of a relationship is also recognised: partnerships displaying above-average bonds and ties will see above-average results. This translates into tangible benefits of better costs, faster transactional processing, higher revenue and better collaboration. This differential may be significant enough to form a competitive advantage for the partners.

Chapter 6
Collaboration Appraisal

Not that old 'if you can't measure it, you manage it' chestnut again!

Introduction

In business, we measure performance in all its forms. The tools used are sophisticated, and people who study for MBAs are required to show an understanding of most of them. Why, then, do we not measure relationship performance? The usual answer is: 'It's too difficult.' Instead, we rely on tracking operational and financial key performance indicators even though these are invariably in arrears and only from our own perspective. We have to trust our partner's figures and guess what is happening across our interfaces. A common problem is that one partner may focus on time, cost and quality, whereas the other will track sales and revenues. Although organisations tie up huge capital and human investments in their strategic alliances, joint ventures and partnerships, they rely heavily on backward-looking, imperfect performance measures. They then wonder how issues that have boiled away unseen, such as complacency, distrust, quality failures, opportunism, late deliveries, cost over-runs and communication gaps, suddenly rear their heads as major issues. Panicked, often the first recourse is to the contract and the penalty clauses.

In a joint operation or enterprise, it is only logical that all sides will have agreed common performance targets as well as coherent individual goals. Performance measurement must therefore be enterprise-wide and become the essential tool for joint collaboration management. If the collaboration is a network or consortium, the appraisal must involve all the partners. Can you answer these simple questions?

- How many business relationships do you have?

- Why are they important?

- Which ones are doing well, and why?

- Which are not doing well, and why?

- What objective measurements can you use?

- How do you identify targets for continuous improvement?

- How do you do all this jointly with your partners?

- How do you do it with minimal effort and maximum effectiveness?

If you were the CEO of a major company looking to take over another, or if you took over the top post of a focal organisation in a supply chain or project management network, are these not the minimum due diligence questions you would need answers to? Having seen the way many blue-chip organisations operate, we can tell you that not only do they not ask them, they do not even know they *need* to ask them. This seems odd, given the so-called scientific management we declare we practice today.

We propose that the answers to these questions are essential if your organisation is involved in collaborative working with others. What is more, we challenge you to get the best out of your strategically critical relationships if you do not have a grip on joint enterprise performance.

What Must the Collaboration Appraisal Do?

Collaboration appraisal needs to fit in with the other metrics that trace time, cost, quality and key events across the boundaries of the partner organisations. They are designed to measure expert perceptions of success in order to highlight opportunities to reap more value from the joint enterprise. The appraisal needs to support a variety of business-to-business relationship functions. As can be seen by the topics covered in the following section, you may be surprised by the extent of appraisal situations that should really form part of relational governance.

- **Survey:**
  - Online questionnaires check key performance measures
  - Knowledgeable people from both companies participate

- **Interview:**
  - No longer than one hour, usually by phone
  - Small number of knowledgeable personnel in each organisation
  - Capture 'headline' views

- **Workshop/report:**
  - Headline 'traffic lights' identify 'what's going on'
  - Interview quotations illustrate graphics – 'why it's happening'
  - Comprehensive conclusions and recommendations
  - Action plan

Figure 6.1   A joint enterprise appraisal process

What Does the Appraisal Process Look Like?

OVERVIEW

The appraisal process should not be complex. It should be easy to carry out, not be disruptive to the participating organisations, the results should be readily understood by staff at all levels, and it should have the buy-in and confidence of all, especially senior management. Figure 6.1 sets out the three simple components of a joint enterprise relationship appraisal: the survey, the interview and the workshop/report.

SETTING

The setting for the appraisal exercise is crucial to its success. Given the sensitivities involved, like marriage guidance counselling, the process must be administered by an independent, impartial, trusted, discreet third party. The supplier is not going to open up if the process is being run by the customer. The third party must be the soul of discretion because the details that will emerge from the appraisal will be commercially sensitive, so a guarantee of complete confidentiality is essential. The appraisal sponsors need to be the participant organisation's relationship managers – senior people who will represent their organisations throughout the process and will be responsible for leading the emergent change programme. The third-party appraisal team will work for them, because it is important that personnel see the process as an internal initiative rather than one that they are being subjected to by outsiders. After all: 'What do outsiders really know about the way we do things?'

Finally, having secured the undivided attention and support of the staff in the organisations participating in the appraisal process, it is very important that once the results have been analysed and presented to the sponsors, comprehensive feedback is arranged. In our experience, these staff will also be extremely keen to become involved in the resultant change programme, and often make excellent change agents.

DATA COLLECTION

All questionnaire respondents must be assured total anonymity and confidentiality in order to secure their open, honest and complete participation. There should be no data collection by workshop as we consider this is a most unreliable way of collecting objective data. If you are sitting next to your boss or your opposite number from a partner organisation, you are likely to hold back from expressing your true views because you do not want to open yourself up to career-limiting honesty, organisational embarrassment or spoil relationships with those you interact with on a regular basis. Instead, semi-structured interviews should be used to add richness to the survey responses – and again, absolute confidentiality must be guaranteed. It is likely that quotations from both the questionnaire comments and the interviews will be used to add impact to the appraisal findings. These must be anonymised to ensure that it is not possible to identify individual contributors or the firms they come from. It is preferable to carry out interviews over the phone. This is less intrusive and time-consuming for interviewees, as well as allowing them to contribute without pressure or distraction. It also enables the interviewer to concentrate more fully on making notes of the key statements made by the interviewee without the need to record and transcribe the conversation.

SURVEY PHASE

Most managers suffer from being bombarded by questionnaires. It is thus vital that this phase minimises the effort required while generating true perceptions of clear, important collaborative relationship issues. To accomplish this, the survey phase consists of a relatively short online questionnaire that is scientifically designed to test the collaboration dynamics that occur between organisations. These questionnaires do not vary, apart from context, regardless of industry sector or setting. The questionnaire should not take more than 15 minutes to complete. It asks for agree/disagree/don't know answers to simple questions that require some thought and provoke respondents to clarify their ideas. As is usual with surveys, there should be a text entry box at the end to allow respondents to freely contribute anything they think is relevant. In one live survey we carried out, a free text entry amounted to eight A4 pages when printed out! Since relationship managers will know their own organisations and staff, they should nominate those who will take part. Establishing a comprehensive sample of knowledgeable people drawn from a wide range of functions and organisational levels will bring in the best-quality data. This is not sampling research, but a self-selected census. As long as the right people with good knowledge are chosen to take part, the number of people surveyed is immaterial.

INTERVIEW PHASE

The purpose of the interviews is to provide the reasoning behind the survey results. Interviewees will be asked to comment on the joint headline traffic light results from the survey. For example:

- Why is this aspect so successful and what is its impact on the joint enterprise? What efforts have been made and could still be made to capitalise on this achievement?

- Why is there such a difference of opinion between the organisations on this particular issue, and how does it affect the way the relationship operates?

- They/you have indicated that this aspect is not performing well. Why? What has been/is being done to overcome the issue?

As long as the right people are selected – those with the roles and seniority who have an overview of both strategic and tactical parts of the relationship – only a small number of interviews will be necessary. Moreover, each session need not take more than an hour to complete.

WORKSHOP PHASE

The joint workshop phase is designed to achieve four things:

1. to endorse the survey and interview findings;

2. to add further richness to the information revealed;

3. to decide and prioritise the actions to be taken;

4. to agree and resource an implementation plan.

The attendees from the participating organisations will include the senior sponsors, often at director level and above, the relationship managers who will take the action programme forward, and the departmental managers and key staff who will be affected. The group must not indulge in finger-pointing and laying the blame at anyone's door, because this is counter-productive. The team must instead face its challenges as a team, and poorly performing areas must be turned around or re-deployed to those who can contribute greater value. It is usually productive to restate and confirm the original alliance value objectives in order to re-establish the motivation for collaboration. Often, these will have been overlooked or forgotten in the hurly-burly of trying to establish and make the relationship work. The overall focus must be joint value-seeking:

- How do we capitalise and further exploit those things we are doing well?

- How do we eliminate waste and turn around dysfunctional processes?

- How do we put in place joint management that aims to continuously improve relationship performance?

- How do we ensure that we seize and capitalise on every new business opportunity that presents itself to the alliance?

IMPLEMENTATION

The implementation plan must be integrated with the joint management of the relationship so that not only does it ensure that what needs to be done gets done, but also that aspiration targets can be set and achieved.

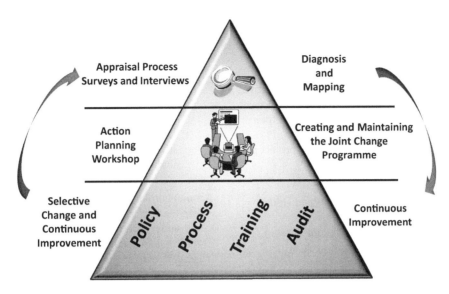

Figure 6.2   The collaborative change cycle

Reactive change initiatives only result in temporary relief from relationship performance decline. This is what we really mean by 'continuous improvement'. Figure 6.2 shows how relationship appraisal dovetails with change implementation to form a continuous improvement cycle. All change must be institutionalised by being incorporated into policy, operational processes and practices, staff training and internal auditing. We usually see this happening in-house, but it is also critical to apply it to the joint management of collaborative relationships.

> *The big shift in focus will be away from price and compliance and toward how organisations address innovation and change through their agreements.*
> *(Bill Huber, Partner, Information Services Group, cited in International Association for Contract and Commercial Management 2012)*

RELATIONSHIP APPRAISAL SUMMARY

Figure 6.3 summarises the key features of the appraisal process. It uses a few academic research expressions because it describes a scientifically based data collection and action research process. At the end of this chapter we provide some more background on the science behind the process.

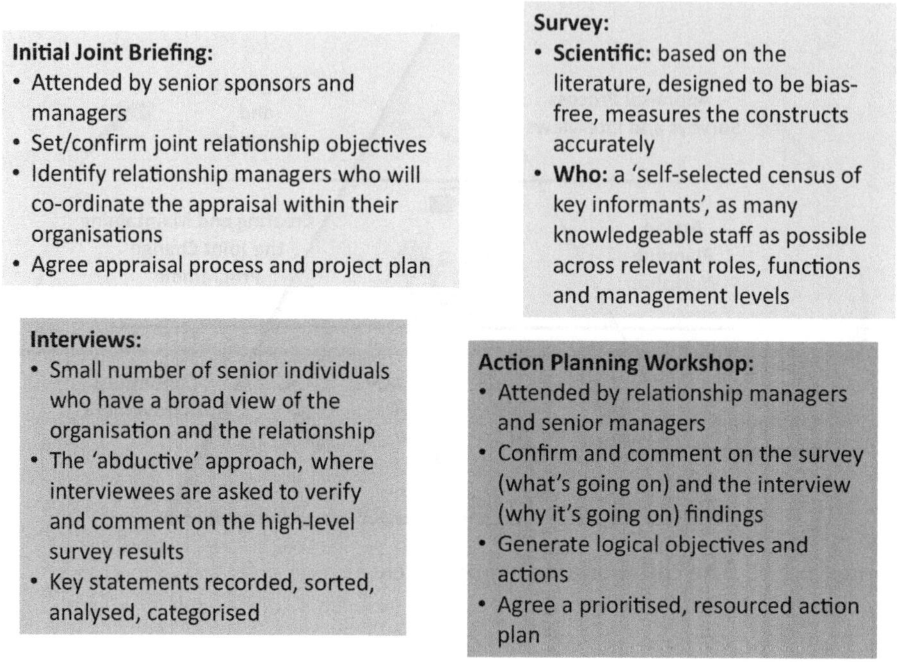

Initial Joint Briefing:
- Attended by senior sponsors and managers
- Set/confirm joint relationship objectives
- Identify relationship managers who will co-ordinate the appraisal within their organisations
- Agree appraisal process and project plan

Survey:
- **Scientific:** based on the literature, designed to be bias-free, measures the constructs accurately
- **Who:** a 'self-selected census of key informants', as many knowledgeable staff as possible across relevant roles, functions and management levels

Interviews:
- Small number of senior individuals who have a broad view of the organisation and the relationship
- The 'abductive' approach, where interviewees are asked to verify and comment on the high-level survey results
- Key statements recorded, sorted, analysed, categorised

Action Planning Workshop:
- Attended by relationship managers and senior managers
- Confirm and comment on the survey (what's going on) and the interview (why it's going on) findings
- Generate logical objectives and actions
- Agree a prioritised, resourced action plan

Figure 6.3   Relationship appraisal key features

The overall aim is to capture and utilise reliable data using a rigorously repeatable method. Moreover, because the data are based on a standard model, it means that the collaborative performance of organisations can be compared and benchmarks applied to make strategic and performance judgements. Thus, senior managers gain a powerful governance tool in a key aspect of business that is not available using traditional methods.

VARIANTS OF RELATIONSHIP APPRAISAL

High-level traffic lights report

Figure 6.4 shows an example of a one-page set of traffic lights that resulted from surveying the views of a pair of partner organisations. The percentage satisfaction scores with the relationship are usually represented by coloured traffic lights and numbers. (The illustrations in this book are in black and white, so in all the artwork, green is represented as grey, green/yellow as light grey, yellow as light shading and red as dark shading.) The performance bandings are defined as follows:

- green (grey) (75–100 per cent) – OK unless high-priority;

- green/yellow (light grey) (65–75 per cent) – corrective action recommended;

- yellow (light) (50–64 per cent) – corrective action required;

- red (dark) (0–49 per cent) – urgent corrective action required.

It is possible to compare the respective perceptions quite easily by focusing on the colours/shades. The main measures are listed on the left, as are the softer aspect such as trust and commitment.

The main measure definitions are as follows:

- **innovation** – the 'leap of faith', being creative, flexible and resilient;

- **investment** – alignment of objectives, investment in people, know-how, infrastructure and management effort and long-term vision;

- **communication** – open and transparent, frequent and extensive learning, planning and anticipating;

- **operations** – focus on service and product delivery, lower joint costs and risks, building trust;

- **value** – perceived and actual benefits – overall relationship satisfaction.

The additional characteristics (softer measures) definitions are as follows:

- **long-term orientation** – promoting continuity, patience and joint gains;

- **interdependence** – encouraging joint responsibility;

- **C3 behaviour** – collaboration, co-operation, co-ordination;

- **trust** – creating goodwill and the incentive to go the extra mile;

Performance at a Glance

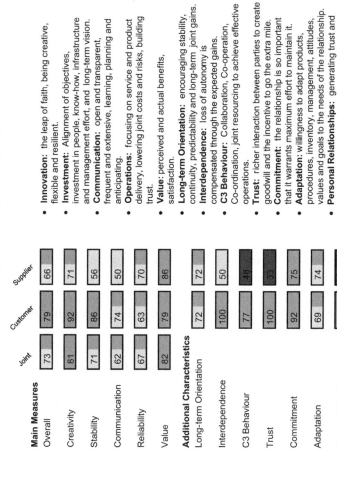

Main Measures

	Joint	Customer	Supplier
Overall	73	79	66
Creativity	81	92	71
Stability	71	86	56
Communication	62	74	50
Reliability	67	63	70
Value	82	79	86

Additional Characteristics

	Customer	Supplier
Long-term Orientation	72	72
Interdependence	100	50
C3 Behaviour	77	48
Trust	100	33
Commitment	92	75
Adaptation	69	74
Personal Relationships	100	44

Bandings	Colour	Response
0-49%	Red	Urgent Action Required
50-59%	Amber	Corrective Action Required
60-74%	Amber/Green	Corrective Action Recommended
75-100%	Green	OK Unless High Priority

- **Innovation:** the leap of faith, being creative, flexible and resilient.
- **Investment:** Alignment of objectives, investment in people, know-how, infrastructure and management effort, and long-term vision.
- **Communication:** open and transparent, frequent and extensive, learning, planning and anticipating.
- **Operations:** focusing on service and product delivery, lowering joint costs and risks, building trust.
- **Value:** perceived and actual benefits, satisfaction.
- **Long-term Orientation:** encouraging stability, continuity, predictability and long-term joint gains.
- **Interdependence:** loss of autonomy is compensated through the expected gains.
- **C3 Behaviour:** Collaboration, Co-operation, Co-ordination, joint resourcing to achieve effective operations.
- **Trust:** richer interaction between parties to create goodwill and the incentive to go the extra mile.
- **Commitment:** the relationship is so important that it warrants maximum effort to maintain it.
- **Adaptation:** willingness to adapt products, procedures, inventory, management, attitudes, values and goals to the needs of the relationship.
- **Personal Relationships:** generating trust and openness through personal interaction.

Figure 6.4   Example of a top-level traffic light report (two-organisation relationship)

- **commitment** – belief that maximum effort should be expended to maintain the partnership;

- **adaptation** – willingness to adapt products, processes, goals and values to sustain the relationship – flexibility;

- **personal relationships** – generating trust, confidence and openness through personal interactions.

The partners in Figure 6.4 were a pair of SMEs, a specialist, electronics company and its parts supplier. It can be seen from the colours of the traffic lights that neither was satisfied with their performance, although the customer was more dissatisfied than the supplier. Their twenty-year relationship had matured into a comfortable 'marriage' where conversations had become mundane grumbles and the innovative spark had died. They had both lost track of each other's changing and improving capabilities, and due to failure to capitalise on the possibilities, were losing their competitive edge. The appraisal came as a wake-up call, and as we can see in the bottom-line figures presented in the list below, they were able to affect a transformation, but good management from the start would have prevented the performance degradation situation from occurring:

- Regular planning meetings defined joint production schedules.

- Joint product reliability action saved £50,000 per year on in-house testing and £90,000 in parts holdings.

- Supplier involvement in new product design brought lower costs, improved design reliability, increased asset availability, improved functionality and shortened time to market from five years to one.

- The customer updated its management information system with new, integrated system to improve asset control, marketing and requirements forecasting.

- Over three years, customer revenue increased 38.5 per cent per year, and supplier revenue increased 35 per cent per year.

Sub-set traffic lights

Focusing on another relationship, Figure 6.5 shows the value dimension from a high-level traffic light report broken down into more detail. It shows the questions asked in the questionnaire and the traffic lights for each. You can see that Firm A feels very strongly that it is trapped in a 'loveless marriage' with doubtful gains. Overall, however, there is a feeling that the relationship has a future and that 'divorce' is not the answer. It turned out that despite satisfactory operational performance, communications between Firm B and Firm A were poor, with format, frequency and method problems resulting in crossed wires and one particularly frustrated partner. It only took a joint review and then realignment of the information channels in this alliance to overcome the issues. More importantly, the appraisal exposed an unexploited opportunity to leverage greater value from the data flows about customer demand trends.

PERSONNEL QUOTATIONS

The traffic lights will give a pretty good view of what is happening in the partnership, or at least where to look. Quotations from the 'additional information' boxes in the questionnaires and the interviews on reactions to the traffic lights will invariably give you the reasons in some detail. The combination of the two provides a very powerful and detailed view of the key performance dynamics in the relationship. The comments staff make have considerable impact, especially on senior staff. They often have an immediacy, freshness and poignancy that bring to the fore the essential issues. Collectively, the quotations can be analysed to show representative perspectives of aspects such as operational process effectiveness, clarity of communications and trustworthiness. During the appraisal workshop phase, the selective use of quotations will reinforce the key messages from the survey data and leave little doubt in the minds of managers about what actions need to be taken. Figure 6.6 shows some examples from a relationship between the UK Ministry of Defence and a major industry partner.

A PORTFOLIO PERSPECTIVE

Figure 6.7 shows a view of 57 relationships between a customer and its main suppliers. The top-level performance figure from each relationship is plotted showing the positive and negative scores (a relationship having an overall satisfaction score of 75 per cent is shown with a green vertical bar for 75 per cent and a red vertical bar for 25 per cent). The horizontal bar spans from green (grey) on the right via green/yellow (light grey) and yellow (light shading) to red (dark shading). These match up with the traffic light colour bandings in Figure 6.4. The colour banding characterisations shown at the bottom of Figure 6.7 have been derived from over 100 major relationships we have researched.

Value

Perceived and actual benefits, satisfaction

		Alliance	Firm A	Firm B
Q5a	The gains – e.g. financial, market, learning – from this relationship are equitably shared between the alliance partners	71	57	86
Q5b	My organisation does not feel imprisoned/restricted within the alliance	40	13	67
Q5c	My organisation is willing to invest more – i.e. money, time, information, effort – in the alliance	94	88	100
Q5d	My organisation is happy that its future is bound to the success of the alliance	81	63	100
Q5e	My organisation feels totally committed to the alliance	94	88	100
Q5f	The alliance is genuinely concerned that my organisation's business succeeds	87	88	86
Q5g	The partners are working to improve the alliance relationships	88	88	89

Figure 6.5   Example of relationship value traffic lights with questions

Customer	Supplier
'We have simple, obvious, open performance measures. Every week the supplier sends us a statement of work achieved, problems and forecasts, and we pass them consumption data. The achievements are open for all to see.'	'If we are to be successful, we must change the perceptions of our customers about us.'
	'Direct access to their data sources such as stocks and forecasts would speed up processes and improve support.'
'Now that we have a partnering arrangement around a good framework contract, we just concentrate on the end customer – we no longer refer to the small print.'	'Our margins are much smaller these days, and this limits the number of people involved in our interface channels. We are having to learn how to make this as effective as possible.'
'Their team had to keep an eye on their commercial man; he had a tendency to go for the small print.'	'A good team is dependent on the mix of individuals. We have been particularly lucky that the people in our joint teams have hit it off so well.'
'They are nice chaps who take us out to lunch, but as an entity they are lacking in service delivery.'	'I would like to repeat this survey over time to see how perceptions change as a result of our joint efforts.'

Figure 6.6   A sample of staff quotations

In Figure 6.7, highlighting the green scores identifies where good practice can be found and red shows where help is needed the most. The customer's portfolio comprised over 200 strategically important relationships. This sample of 54 included small, medium and very large alliances that were felt to be representative of the complete set.

In this case, the customer's head office working with its own and the suppliers' managers generated a catalogue of best practices and practitioners from its best relationships. It then ran a couple of projects using these resources to support and mentor a very poor and a medium relationship. The aim was not only to change the 'game', but also to pilot an approach that could be rolled out across the portfolio with the intention of standardising the approach to relationship management. This plan also allowed the targeting of corporate-level resources on prevalent issues such as complex technological environments (engineering), retaining and motivating staff with critical skills (human resources), standardising collaborative contracts (commercial), improving knowledge-sharing (IT) and consignment/item tracking (supply chain).

Finally, the group CEO met with the industry steering group's leaders and decided that the portfolio perspective provided a new governance opportunity.

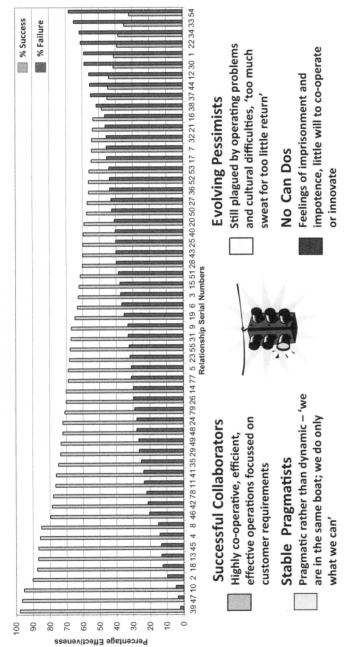

Figure 6.7   A portfolio of procurement and technical support project relationships in order of descending performance

It would allow the group to set performance targets for the portfolio as a whole that would cascade down via corporate directors to the individual project relationships.

THE CONSORTIUM PERSPECTIVE

Figure 6.8 shows how an appraisal can be used to understand the relationship dynamics within a multi-party alliance or consortium that has common objectives. The same measures are used as for the two-party relationship described in Figure 6.4, but in this case staff from each organisation completed the questionnaire so that it is possible to contrast the views of the participating organisations.

In this case, six organisations were involved. The Borough Council was distinctly nervous about its Children's Policy, Health was concerned, Education was not too bothered, Criminal Justice was complacent, and the two Housing Charities felt that nobody cared. Following the interview phase, at the action planning workshop the parties saw that their end-to-end processes were not working properly because they did not have defined owners or performance targets. Moreover, although the teamwork was enthusiastic, it was not effective. They agreed to:

- map the end-to-end processes for each service;

- review the performance requirements of each process;

- review the staff training and policy needs for each process;

- establish a process manager for each process to serve as the main point of contact for its operational delivery;

- upgrade the information flows so that all members receive timely, accurate communications;

- establish a regular alliance management group with its terms of reference and standard agenda;

- introduce a team-building programme;

- carry out further alliance performance appraisals annually.

Alliance Performance at a Glance

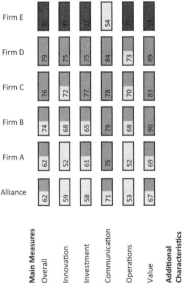

Figure 6.8   Performance traffic light set for a public sector alliance

Conclusions

This chapter has demonstrated how joint relationship performance appraisal has an essential role to play in your formal enterprise relationship management practices. These benefits are highly relevant and tangible as they:

- serve as the catalyst for defining joint opportunities to increase revenue and shareholder value;

- increase customer satisfaction from better product/service quality and delivery;

- strengthen the bond between partners and enhance their ability to innovate;

- reduce administration and production costs and risks;

- bridge the hidden gaps in teamwork through greater cohesion, integration and fulfilment, and increased transparency;

- build joint capabilities to seize future business opportunities.

We have looked at well over 100 major inter-organisational relationships, and we have seen these sorts of outcomes time after time. So maybe there is still some truth in the adage: 'If you can't measure it, you can't manage it!'

THE SCIENCE OF COLLABORATION APPRAISAL

The core of any scientific theory is a theoretical model, and scientific research methods that test the model using real-world data. The relationship appraisal process we have described in this chapter is based on the work of the Nobel Prize winning US economist Oliver Williamson (1975). He suggested that firms had three choices: to do the work in-house, to work co-operatively with partners or to go out into the market to buy the goods and services they needed. The conditions for deciding which course of action to take are shown in Figure 6.9, with one aspect – asset specificity – broken out on the left to give you a flavour of its terms. Basically, firms and public sector organisations tend to keep core functions in-house because they are their most valuable assets (however, we will explore the risks of getting this decision wrong in Chapter 7). The things you buy in the market are uncomplicated and available from multiple sources.

'Make, Collaborate or Buy?'

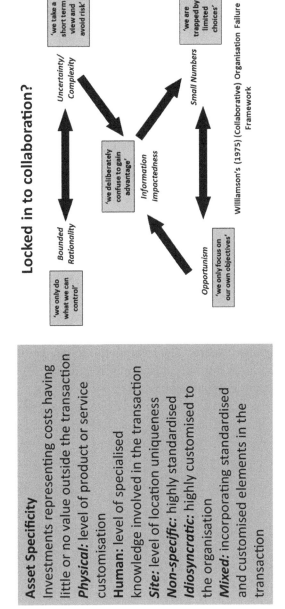

Hierarchical governance	Relational governance	Market governance
High asset specificity	Medium asset specificity	Low asset specificity
High uncertainty/complexity	Medium uncertainty/complexity	Low uncertainty/complexity
Infrequent transactions	Medium transactions level	Frequent transactions
High opportunism	Medium opportunism	Low opportunism

Locked in to collaboration?

'we take a short term view and avoid risk'

'we are trapped by limited choices'

Uncertainty/ Complexity

Small Numbers

'we deliberately confuse to gain advantage'

Information Impactedness

Bounded Rationality

'we only do what we can control'

Opportunism

'we only focus on our own objectives'

Williamson's (1975) (Collaborative) Organisation Failure Framework

Asset Specificity
Investments representing costs having little or no value outside the transaction
Physical: level of product or service customisation
Human: level of specialised knowledge involved in the transaction
Site: level of location uniqueness
Non-specific: highly standardised
Idiosyncratic: highly customised to the organisation
Mixed: incorporating standardised and customised elements in the transaction

Figure 6.9 Transaction cost economics – why organisations collaborate

Collaboration is all about working with others for mutual gain to produce goods or services that neither of you could provide alone.

The little model on the right of Figure 6.9 shows what can happen if you become locked in to a relationship and insufficient effort has been devoted to managing it. This situation usually creeps up on the partners over time, by which point they have intertwined their business processes, investments and staff to such an extent that breaking up is almost unthinkable. The disruption to customers and suppliers as well as business continuity usually forces them to remain in a less than productive partnership. That very negative model is the extreme end of the spectrum, and it is of course possible to find relationships – like marriages – that are made in heaven.

The 'locked in to collaboration' model in Figure 6.9 can be resolved into the negative feedback loop shown on the left in Figure 6.10, where, unless action is taken to interrupt the worsening situation, relationship value will plummet. The other end of the spectrum, where 'one good thing leads to another' and value is continually created, is shown on the right. The appraisal method we have described discovers where a relationship fits between the negative and positive feedback spirals. Questionnaire data are recorded and processed to provide perception percentage ratings in traffic light form. The questionnaire comments plus interview quotations are then analysed. Together they support the production of performance reports that are used as the basis for joint management action. The total methodology is thus capable of appraising any collaborative inter-organisational relationship in order to reveal its detailed performance dynamics.

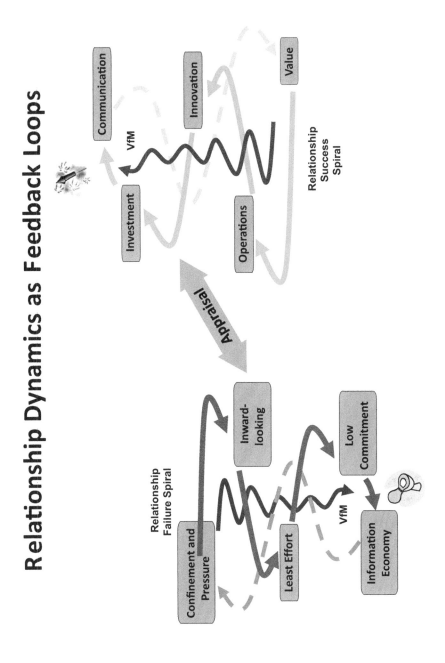

Figure 6.10   Positive and negative relationship spirals

Chapter 7

From Cost to Value Creation in Outsourcing and Facilities Management Relationships

Introduction

Earlier in this book we described the impact of complexity and culture on the management of business-to-business relationships. In particular, we mentioned the need to adopt specific, collaborative networking strategies in order to adapt most readily to changing opportunities. We also examined the elements that constitute the success drivers: relationship management, collaborative innovation, partnership quality and value creation. We described relationship dynamics spirals as a means of understanding the key organisational performance drivers. This chapter brings together aspects of these topics in discussing a prevalent conundrum of today's alliance management: how are global organisations evolving outsourcing and facilities management relationships from cost reduction to value creation?

Outsourcing and facilities management services are big business. Gartner forecasted for 2013 that the global market for information technology outsourcing alone would reach $288 billion – an increase of 2.8 per cent compared to the previous year.[1] MBD (2014) found that in 2012 the UK facilities management business was worth £106.3 billion, with an estimated increase to £117.2 billion by 2017. Governments around the world are looking to facilities management to move functions out of the public sector and to achieve cost savings as well as value-for-money improvements. As the market becomes more competitive, pressure increases on firms to deliver benefits that go beyond cost reductions into value-adding areas such as innovation, responsiveness and resilience. To obtain these capability advantages, organisations have to look at suppliers

---

1   Gartner (2013) 'Gartner Says Worldwide IT Outsourcing Market to Reach $288 Billion in 2013'. Press release, 17 July: www.gartner.com/newsroom/id/2550615 (accessed 28 November 2013).

more strategically and make changes to their relational arrangements and governance mechanisms.

The Business Model

Outsourcing is a business model whereby an organisation decides that it will no longer carry out a function in-house. Instead, this function will be provided by a third party. Outsourced functions could include manufacturing, IT, accounting and logistics. In the context of IT services, outsourcing has been defined as the process of contracting-out or selling the organisation's IT assets, staff and/or activities (including infrastructure, applications and business processes) to a third-party supplier which in exchange provides and manages IT assets and services for monetary return over an agreed period. Facilities management uses the same business rationale, but tends to be more focused on buildings management and maintenance, catering, an extensive range of security services, and health and safety. However, in recent times it has moved into areas such as environmental stewardship, procurement, human resources and payroll services, and real estate management. It is quite common at contract let for resources such as personnel and facilities to be transferred to the provider in both functions. There is thus a growing overlap between them, to the extent that it might be said that outsourcing and facilities management have much the same character.

The decision to outsource or employ managed services is based on business imperatives such as concentration on core activities, cost savings, risk mitigation and access to resources. Many studies point out that the primary motivation is cost reduction, and this was certainly the initial driver for off-shoring call centres. The actual experience of many organisations has been that cost reductions from using cheap labour have been short-lived because wage inflation in countries such as India has reduced the cost advantage. Moreover, service quality has always been difficult to maintain due to language, cultural and governance difficulties, the problem of dealing with overseas call centres has entered into public legend, and the sustainable sourcing issues in the clothing sector have had an adverse impact on major retailers' reputations. It is difficult and costly to keep moving operations from one country to another – note the tendency to near-shore and even re-shore! However, as experience has built up, there has been a recognition that outsourcing and facilities management can add value through accessing specialised partner resources including skills and expertise, process improvement, rapid problem-solving, flexibility, demand management and knowledge creation. Thus, firms have decided that they will create value through global outsourcing – a phenomenon known as strategic outsourcing – and in the facilities management arena, total facilities management contracts.

How Far Do You Go?

There has been a noticeable tendency for organisations to go beyond outsourcing business processes such as call centres and manufacturing, extending the practice to knowledge-based intellectual activities such as product design and R&D. This trend became increasingly visible during the 1990s, when companies such as IBM began to outsource not just manufacturing, but also design activities. It reached its peak within the past decade, when even companies such as Boeing and Hyundai started outsourcing innovation activities. This leads to the question of how far outsourcing strategies should go. Is there a danger that companies become too dependent on outside suppliers and surrender too much control? What happens when your suppliers gain a better technological understanding of your products than you have? What happens when you lose control over the overall design concept that incorporates your knowledge of customer requirements which your suppliers don't have? What happens when you then lose the capability to integrate components into a quality end product? What happens if something goes wrong and you no longer have the skills and knowledge to reintegrate the services or functions into your organisation? Some major manufacturing organisations have not realised that they have lost critical control until they experience reduced sales, increases in product failures and recalls, or a failure of vital services such as IT and payroll.

In the early 1990s, a major automotive company with over 3,000 components suppliers began increasing the amount of design work it expected them to do. From the mid-1990s, complete systems were outsourced. Reducing direct relationships to 350 key systems suppliers would decrease integration, increase flexibility, reduce lead times, cut development costs and improve product quality by making greater use of suppliers' skills and knowledge. As a result, many of the company's experienced engineers left to work for the systems suppliers, and gradually some suppliers began integrating large parts of the vehicles.

In the end, the automotive company did not become involved in integrating the main components of its vehicles until many of the most important decisions impacting performance had been made, at which point, undoing them was difficult and costly. Late changes were not only complicated and expensive, but also led to delays in product launches. Moreover, it meant that products could not be tested fully, which often led to assembly problems or product recalls.

By 2005, it was realised that the outsourcing strategy had seriously weakened the firm's technical competency. Efforts to bring key design functions back into the firm are still continuing today.

It has been proposed that companies should keep activities in-house if they have direct impacts on product performance, and they should maintain control over activities that impact on the performance of the overall product or service. This advice is theoretically correct, but the costs of maintaining these capabilities over the long term may well exceed the benefits of using outside providers. Moreover, it may be impossible to implement as an expedient solution in the case of sudden and serious service disruptions. These risks need to be factored into organisations' collaborative, complexity strategies.

Transitioning Outsourcing and Facilities Management Relationships

One model suggests there are five key stages in the outsourcing process (see Figure 7.1). The first two stages involve identifying the activities to outsource (1) and the selection of the outsourcee (2). These lead to the contractual stage (3), where the governance mechanisms are formalised and the key performance parameters are defined. The signing of the contracts initiates the management stages, where performance is measured and monitored (4) and the relationship is managed (5).

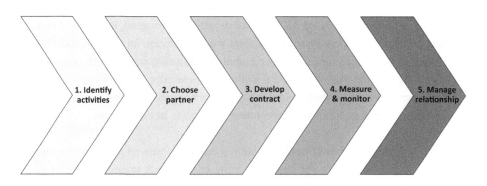

Figure 7.1   The outsourcing process

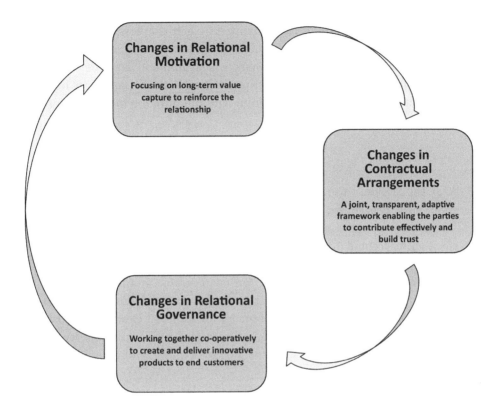

Figure 7.2   A Transitional Governance Process Model

Much attention has focused on the outsourcing decision (stages 1 and 2) or on the outcomes of the process (stage 4), with an emphasis on the role of the outsourcer. However, many companies have discovered that the success of an outsourcing/facilities management venture is determined by the operational effectiveness of the client–supplier relationship. When the relationship is treated as being collaborative, this emphasis assumes overwhelming importance. Our research shows that rather than being a linear process, the transition from cost to value creation is cyclical (see Figure 7.2).

This is also an intuitive deduction, because it is well known that trust and co-operation are not suddenly gained, but have to be earned through repeated and increasingly important transactions. The model relies on continuous adaptation by the partners, both in terms of how they work together as an effective team and how they adapt to changes in their environment. It has three components: contractual, relational and motivational alignments that influence each other in a positive, reinforcing manner. In later chapters we will explain in some detail the practicalities of relationship management, including using ERM as a formal approach, performance measurement, and the interplay between contracts and relational governance. We will thus concentrate here on the role value capture plays in sustaining and building the motivation of the relationship partners.

A global facilities management company was contracted to support a government department with over 250 regional service delivery locations. The client was under great pressure to save money and to increase its efficiency. It accepted that there would be considerable cultural obstacles from the workforce, but it was felt that collaborative working would overcome the difficulties. The service provider had not operated in a large multi-site environment before, and budgeted to instigate a total facilities management approach as soon as possible. This meant, for instance, that cleaning and other services would only be carried out when necessary rather than on a regular schedule.

After a year, the relationship was in difficulties. Delays in understanding the service requirements of the numerous delivery locations, problems with staff acceptance of the new environment, cost overruns due to the need to employ more staff for longer than planned, the escalation of even small problems to senior level and, growing impatience by directors on both sides were bringing into question the whole contract. It was clear from the outset that neither side fully understood how collaboration would work in practice, and the 'big bang' implementation gave the partners no opportunity to build trust, confidence and effective service delivery.

Blurred Perceptions

Time and again we have seen boards announce a collaborative alliance in order to pull off a 'magical marriage'. They bid for contracts that were previously out of reach, put products on the shelves at a fraction of the cost of their competitors, dream up a new product which will corner the market, and provide a service package well beyond anything they have ever done before. Two years later, when none of these objectives have been achieved, they have no idea why things have gone wrong. From our perspective, there is a gulf between these grandiose views of collaborative value and the ability of management to translate these into achievable goals. Even in the largest companies there seems to be a failure to understand that collaboration means pooling resources and working together to achieve objectives that neither party could attain on their own. This calls for whole new views of what value is, how it is created and how it is captured.

Value Contents

Most will probably see value as the achievement of increased profits, greater market share and the fulfilment of project objectives. These will be underpinned by operational imperatives of time, cost, quality and delivery. However, there is more to value than this. A number of intangible factors will also come into play, such as innovation, knowledge and skills capture, enhanced reputation and brand value, and satisfied stakeholders. More difficult to quantify, but equally important as an enabler, is relationship quality. This is characterised by harmony, trust, commitment, open communications and a willingness to work together over the long term. Altogether, these value components will have short- and long-term aspects, and because of the nature of collaboration, there will be aspirational, potential and emergent opportunities that will have an impact.

When companies start working collaboratively, they often begin with specific aims. These will take into account the known capabilities of both partners. As they move forward, further abilities will become evident. More open and in-depth communication will occur, creativity and innovation will be stimulated, and the partners will broaden their focus to include these and 'up their game'. Suddenly, ideas that were vague dreams become achievable. This provides impetus for joint investment that enables the partners to seize unforeseen opportunities as they arise. It is this enhanced capability of the partnership which forms the potential aspect of collaborative value. It becomes a method of working that is capable of continuous value creation as the quality of the relationship improves. Therefore, the partners must expect that unforeseen value opportunities will emerge, and must be prepared to manage their creation and exploitation. Thus, contrary to some traditional views that collaborative relationships can be established immediately simply by having the right partner selection process and signing the contract, it is clear that collaborative working, value creation and value capture develop in an increasingly productive cycle, as shown in Figure 7.3. This resembles the Partnering Behaviour Success Spiral described in Chapter 5.

The new framework contract runs for five years at a fixed cost. This gives us guaranteed service availability and a 20 per cent reduction in costs. The Supplier is incentivised to be innovative and increase equipment reliability. In return, he can plan his workload more effectively, cut overheads and home in on fault trends.

(UK Ministry of Defence helicopter project manager)[2]

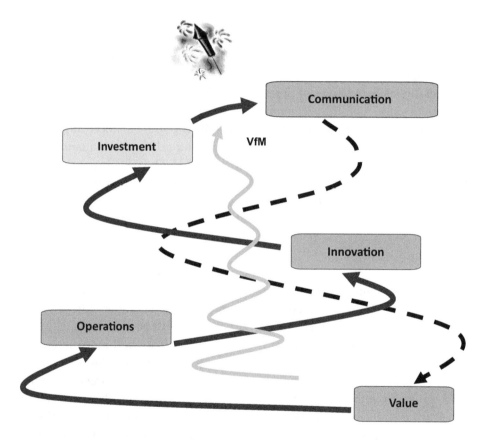

Figure 7.3   The Continuous Value Creation Cycle

---

2   All the quotations interspersed with the text of this chapter are responses from participants in the authors' research.

Broken Cycles

Seventy-five per cent of alliances fail to live up to expectations because they do not enter the Continuous Value Creation Cycle. There are many reasons for this, but overall, the lack of clear focus on what the value proposition is and how it is to be achieved leads to unreality in the ways the relationships develop. The partners will inevitably have different views, and if these are not reconciled into a joint one from the start, then the divergence of objectives will sow the seeds of relationship failure.

> *We have been struggling for over two years to make this partnership work. Staff at all levels are frustrated by our inability to work together more productively. It has recently dawned upon us that this might be because we didn't re-negotiate the contract when we decided to become collaborative.*
>
> *(Global IT outsourcer)*

There are a number of common situations where the Continuous Value Creation Cycle is interrupted and value is lost:

- **Not adapting to change** – New requirements are not recognised and reconciled, so a gulf opens up between the partners.

> *We couldn't change the relationship to access the supplier's wider expertise therefore we terminated it and looked for a new one where we could.*
>
> *(IT outsourcer)*

> *We want to deliver a Total Facilities Management Service but the customer just wants cleaners and security guards.*
>
> *(Global facilities management service provider)*

- **Level blockers** – The board may well be in agreement about the benefits of collaboration, but failure to communicate this clearly to the various levels in their organisation leads to staff feeling threatened by the requirement for a more co-operative approach and resisting the development of the relationship.

> *I know what they want, but it's too airy-fairy for a construction company. You try and be nice, and the customer jumps all over you.*
>
> *(Chief engineer, global construction company)*

- **Value confusion** – Relationship disharmony is confused with poor relationship performance, which reduces the perception of the value generated. This could result in a highly productive relationship failing.

We hate working with them but we can't find anybody else who does the job better.

(Global food manufacturer)

- **Feelgood/complacency** – This is the 'party culture', where the relationship has settled into a cosy groove where 'inconveniences' such as financial governance and process improvements are ignored. Poor performance is masked by good intentions and high activity. Value capture is subordinated to an easy ride, and things start to go south when the bills come in.

We built them a terrific electricity sub-station but unfortunately it flooded the first time it rained. They still paid us for it though, and the re-work.

(Power engineering sub-contractor, national construction project)

- **Bad targets** – If you continue to lay year-on-year price reductions on your supplier, does this incentivise it to work collaboratively? Or if a partner maximises its efficiency at the expense of the other, is this good teamwork?

They just dump these precision instruments on the dockside with no protective packaging because they are keen to go on leave after their voyage. We are only contracted to service the things but then get hammered by their commercial people for charging the extra to fix them because they are broken.

(Major UK defence contractor)

- **The seized cycle** – Innovation in the relationship has ceased, and the partners have become dependent on each other rather than interdependent. Due to market factors, they are unable to find a replacement for each other and have to 'stay together for the sake of the kids'.

- **Out of touch** – Value capture has slowed because one of the partners has failed to stay aware of the other's increasing skills, knowledge and capability.

The reason why we have been struggling to launch a new product is because we are wedded to old technology. We have just found out that our partner can supply far more capable modern components.
(SME electronics designer/manufacturer)

- **Unrealised dreams** – The partners are unable to convert the dream into reality. Because they fail to understand the full potential of the relationship, they devote insufficient effort to make it work and they are unable to capitalise on its potential and opportunities.

We felt they weren't trying so we went off to talk to a competitor. Unfortunately they found out.
(IT vendor/vendor partner)

Post-mortem: The Struggles to Realise Value

Based upon a number of major cases we have been involved with over the last 15 years, the following sequence portrays how lack of appreciation of collaborative value results in a struggling relationship.

The boards of the partners decide that there is considerable value in adopting a collaborative relationship. In particular, tapping into the wider capabilities of the partners will enable more innovative ways of working, leading to lower costs and greater efficiency.

At this point, they assume that their senior management will define what is meant by 'working collaboratively', and will identify the commercial and operational changes that are needed to secure the desired value. Unfortunately, this expectation is often not fulfilled.

Senior management meet with the commercial managers and the sales staff. Not realising that they need to explore a completely new way of working with their opposite numbers, they hammer out a revised contract. This looks very much like the old one, but incorporates the increased requirements they think the new, closer relationship should deliver, with the additional governance clauses needed to manage it. Usually, because their focus is on the bottom line there is minimal or reduced investment, with, for example, a demand for a year-on-year 5 per cent price reduction.

The new contract then hits the operational levels like a bolt from the blue. It contains expectations that they are either unable to satisfy or require considerable changes to implement – and often with cost penalties. Furthermore, there is no plan for the realignment of the organisations to make a new way of joint working possible. As a result, staff increase their work rate in fruitless pursuit of the new targets. Frustration and friction levels inevitably rise and adversely affect performance. Eventually, penalty clauses are threatened and the commercial managers get involved.

Increased innovation is a significant expectation of this contract, although it does not specify how it is to be incentivised or rewarded. Furthermore, new communications channels to discuss innovative value creation and value capture are not established. At the operations levels, frenzied activity and performance issues leave very little scope or appetite for developing and implementing new ideas.

After a while, it is evident that the collaboration is not delivering the value envisaged, and the boards begin to question the original concept. The fact that the collaboration initiative was not implemented is not recognised as the source of failure. This top-level doubt starts to permeate into the alliance organisations.

The customer company was one of the top UK financial services companies. The supplier was a global organisation specialising in consulting and outsourcing with many blue-chip customers. The original purpose of the relationship was staff support and provision of additional capacity, with little opportunity for increased scope. However, following the economic downturn, this gradually expanded to include managed services, with further expectations of a strategic nature. However, the transition from a cost-focused to a value-focused relationship was taking place in a haphazard way, without much investment, and thus achieving only marginal results.

The expectations of the relationship were changing, and the new requirements were yet to be fully articulated. While the supplier prided itself on providing efficient and reliable products, the customer expected a bespoke service. This led to misalignment between the partners in terms of business understanding, objectives and commercial opportunity. In particular, there was a need to define knowledge-sharing and innovation processes in order to take advantage of industry and technology opportunities. It also required a change to collaborative management from both partners, involving clearer leadership and engagement with the staff.

'We have not had an open conversation about account objectives in two years, so there is no context for how we can help each other.'

At the operational level, new aspirations and changes to ways of working have been communicated, but have not yet embedded as common practice across the organisation, so unhelpful behaviours such as over-analysis, tight control and insufficient information-sharing continue. Moreover, there were some indications of team integration issues due to cultural differences. In a collaborative working pilot programme, both partners were defining and implementing the changes co-operatively and learning from the experience.

'We are missing a formal cascade to all contractors and organisations of the customer's business context; we have to rely on informal discussions and office rumours.'

This is a relationship that had evolved through working together more closely over time. The customer decided that it was appropriate to adopt a more collaborative approach, because it 'felt right' and because other companies in the financial services industry sector were doing likewise. Although the supplier was happy with the plan, both partners failed to agree what would happen differently. The normal business continued as usual, but expectations of 'exciting prospects' did not materialise. The result was growing dissatisfaction, especially at the operational level, and frustration at the lack of new communication channels seen as vital to enable the relationship to progress. At the senior level, the customer felt that the supplier's performance had deteriorated despite the fact that his detailed satisfaction of the service level agreement at a customary high level had been maintained. As a result, the supplier felt that his efforts to accommodate the customer's increased expectations were not understood or appreciated. The lack of a new joint business framework was severely impeding the efforts to establish a collaborative relationship, and in particular trust was being undermined.

Savvy organisations that 'do it right' from the start will develop a robust relationship which is capable of producing high returns today and a long-term revenue stream. However, those that take a limited view of value will not. In our experience, they really do not understand what value means for both partners, how they capture it, and how they will continue to take advantage of new prospects. They thus fail to put in place a collaborative management structure and environment that establishes and enters them into the Continuous Value Creation Cycle. The relationship becomes fractious, innovation does not happen, and productivity is only average at best. The investment underperforms and customers are disappointed. Currently, this happens far too often, and viable alliance opportunities are wasted.

Conclusions

It is plainly apparent that outsourcing and facilities management relationships face particular problems in transitioning from traditional cost-seeking to value creation. The solution of these issues is of critical importance, since these forms of business are growing ever more important as firms seek to 'stick to their knitting' and buy rather than own important functions. Many have tried the cost-reduction route of transactional relationships, and some are starting to give up, having discovered that capturing collaborative value remains extremely difficult. Nevertheless, a persistent few have realised that if only they can discover the formula, there are considerable gains to be made that go well beyond those that could be achieved working on their own. It seems that the greatest barrier is realising that collaboration means working very closely together. In facilities management, the service provider is usually under the same roof, and more often than not firmly embedded in the customer's organisation. Despite this closeness, the service provider is often treated as a functionary whose extended capabilities are not recognised. In the case of outsourcers, they struggle to maintain or improve quality at a distance, and in many cases in the face of very different cultures. Sustainable sourcing and environmental traceability are also concerns, especially when dealing with supply chains in developing countries. The success formula appears to be tied to the realisation that that the transition process is cyclical to enable the partners to get to know each other and to understand how they can work together effectively. ERM is a key factor because it provides the governance arrangements to support this. A vital component is the Continuous Value Creation Cycle, because of its reciprocal impact on motivation. This is based on the joint understanding of what the relationship's value actually is – both now and potentially in the future. As long as this alignment is continuously updated, then realism reigns and the partners can combine their resources to capture the maximum possible value.

Chapter 8

Principles of Collaboration Management: A Formal Discipline

We have previously described the value of having a coherent network strategy as one of the two enablers to achieve collaborative success. This chapter concentrates on the second: the principles of managing collaborative relationships. Enterprise relationship management is the process for co-ordinating all the business processes and activities that are essential to the success of a joint/multi-party endeavour, and is structured around a three-phase approach: a Decision Phase, an Operations Phase and an Exit Phase. It involves the formal management of those aspects of a joint enterprise that contribute to the bottom line by blending together framework contracting and relational governance (see Figure 8.1). The practical aspects of how to do this are covered in Chapter 9.

Management Confusion

It is worrying that for many businesses, their key relationships are managed and developed in an ad hoc manner, with the individuals responsible for supporting business-critical relationships receiving little guidance and support. Moreover, responsibility for this key function is usually distributed (and dissipated) across the organisation, with no overall perspective of performance. Perhaps the salesman who won the deal is keen to ensure that the client is happy and will be inclined to offer him the next deal. The operations manager has to ensure that the day-to-day business runs smoothly. The commercial manager keeps a weather eye on the contract to ensure that delivery is in accordance with the specification. The managing director has an annual game of golf with his counterparts in his major customers to ensure they are happy and to glean opportunities for the future. But where is the overview of this relationship, checking its efficient use of resources, controlling and monitoring performance, solving problems and embracing innovation, and seeing and seizing the new opportunities created by the joint enterprise?

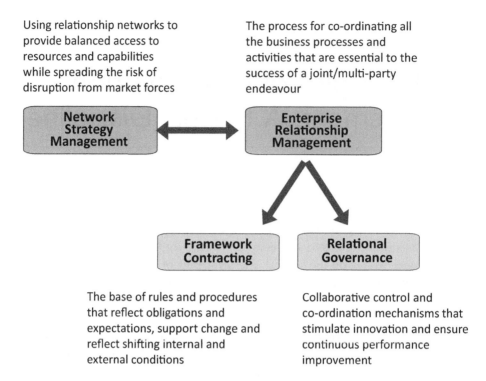

Using relationship networks to provide balanced access to resources and capabilities while spreading the risk of disruption from market forces

The process for co-ordinating all the business processes and activities that are essential to the success of a joint/multi-party endeavour

The base of rules and procedures that reflect obligations and expectations, support change and reflect shifting internal and external conditions

Collaborative control and co-ordination mechanisms that stimulate innovation and ensure continuous performance improvement

Figure 8.1   Framework for Collaborative Success

How are the internal processes in each organisation optimised to focus on each partner without conflicts or gaps? Such a lack of overall control engenders an atmosphere of helplessness, a tendency to be surprised by unexpected problems, diminishing trust and leading to a readiness to 'reach for the contract'.

It is no wonder that managing business alliances is often seen as a black art where we don't know what to do, we don't know that we don't know what to do, it's somebody else's job, or we haven't the time or money to do it. In order to manage, goals need to be set and resources have to be utilised effectively to achieve the overall objective. Few companies set relationship goals, and even fewer measure and monitor the rich resource of relationships they have. Many businesses have no formal process for developing and managing relationships. Our education system often emphasises the technical skills of operating within a business, devoting little time to developing the relational skills. This, it can be argued, increases the risk profile of the organisation and its network of partners, and its likelihood to under-perform or fail.

The Case for Relationship Management

You will be very familiar with the core business disciplines of finance, contracts, manufacturing, human resources, sales, marketing and supply chain management. But would you be surprised if we told you that the overwhelming proportion of very significant business relationships have inadequate collaboration management? Many of these organisations are household names, global entities with multi-billion-dollar turnovers. Moreover, they depend heavily on the services and products of strategic partners for their competitive and operational success. How many times have you seen collaboration management fall vaguely between the supplier relationship and key account management functions? Each of these strongly advocates a relational approach. However, each inevitably comes from either the supplier's (time, cost and quality) or the buyer's (sales and revenue) perspective. We maintain that organisations which try to manage collaborative relationships in this way will develop crossed wires and experience difficulty meeting in the middle. At the very minimum, the friction and inefficient engagement between partners within relationship networks will create an additional 15 per cent cost overhead, and more often than not, considerably more. It is thus not surprising that the prime cause of alliance failure and low performance is poor collaboration management.

Today, with the preponderance of network-enabled enterprise as the competitive business model, whether you are an SME, a complex, tiered structure of construction companies or a far-reaching supply chain network, there is an overriding need to formalise the approach to managing and developing collaborative business relationships. This does not come for free: quality management comes at a significant cost. Nevertheless, it is time that senior managers realised that considerable, short- and long-term benefits are there for the taking. These will make the difference between success and mediocrity. We recognise that all relationships are different and so are their configurations, but there are common building blocks that can be used. This has also been recognised by the issue of the British Standard 11000 on Collaborative Business Relationships, which comprehensively defines steps to establish and improve collaborative relationships.

The Payback from Relationship Management

We have already established that collaborative networks require resources and time to develop and maintain, but the dividends are correspondingly great.

Effective relationship management will therefore aim to establish strong joint governance procedures that ensure good communications and early warning systems. This will incentivise the parties to work together to reduce the probability of risk and failure that would normally be a standard part of doing business with other organisations. It will allow them to be jointly proactive and innovative in dealing with uncertainty and new business opportunities where they will be able to focus on service and product delivery, lowering joint costs and risks, and building and sustaining trust.

Having a commercial agreement that provides a flexible framework will avoid the need for onerous penalties, and moreover, robust relational governance will provide mechanisms for regular communications, reviews and mutual performance assessments. These factors blend together into enterprise relationship management, which creates a holistic management system that is capable of catering for all forms of collaborative activity. Successful relationship-building will include joint projects or initiatives that cause the parties to focus on continuous improvement or innovation, thereby enhancing mutual value. The benefits of the partnering arrangement are that firms are future-proofed, uncertainty is removed, managers can plan, and everyone can really focus on the customer.

The Importance of a Management Framework

The traditional approach to managing performance often results in the saw-tooth effect shown in Figure 8.2.

Every so often you address the problem with consultants, and if you are lucky there is a dramatic increase in performance. However, this soon starts to wear off and the intervention has to be repeated. If you are not careful, the dips will be exaggerated by the loss of demoralised staff. A number of management initiatives such as quality standards and balanced scorecards have been employed to get over this syndrome and onto a 'continuous improvement' path. There is no reason why collaborative performance should not do the same, but it will require initiatives specifically targeted at enterprise relationship management. In today's markets, where internal and external challenges abound, companies cannot afford to ignore a principle that will secure them a competitive edge.

The Importance of Planning

Figure 8.2   Relationship management for continuous improvement

You will recognise the standard 'Plan, Do, Check, Act' cycle. Relationship management principles use a slightly different virtuous circle that acknowledges the joint nature of the endeavour. The partners first review the performance of their collaborative relationship and its achievements. They then consider the problems that inhibit their performance and the opportunities that are available to them. Next, they agree the improvements to their processes and behaviours that will enhance their ability to work together effectively. Finally, they incorporate these changes into their standard operating procedures, policies and training. In this way, continuous improvement is achieved and performance improvements become inevitable.

BS 11000 is very comprehensive and complex, so we will focus on simplifying the approach because it is likely to be more memorable, easier to adopt and scalable for organisations of all sizes. The three phases of both approaches are shown in Figure 8.3 for comparison. The process of relationship management is often represented as being linear, but of course it is iterative, and can be entered or re-entered at any point.

Two Formal Management Approaches

Simplified	BS 11000
The Decision Phase: *selecting new partners on collaborative principles*	**Stage 1 – Awareness:** *strategic policies and processes leading to collaborative working* **Stage 2 – Knowledge:** *developing a business case and implementation strategy for an identified opportunity* **Stage 3 – Internal Assessment:** *capability and maturity to successfully engage in collaboration* **Stage 4 – Partner Selection:** *evaluating capabilities and skills to bring complementary strengths to the relationship, and identifying whether aims and objectives can be synchronised*
The Operations Phase: *the robust, joint management structures for managing a collaborative relationship throughout its productive life, ensuring efficiency, effectiveness resilience and continuous performance improvement*	**Stage 5 – Working Together:** *establishing executive sponsorship, operational structure, governance, roles and responsibilities to achieve the business objectives* **Stage 6 – Value Creation:** *operational performance improvement, resource optimisation, process enhancement, waste and cost reduction* **Stage 7 – Staying Together:** *monitoring and measuring performance and the relationship, ensuring that it remains focused on the agreed business objectives*
The Exit Phase: *carefully planned and managed to ensure a satisfactory outcome for all stakeholders, retaining goodwill and the opportunity to do business in the future, learning from experience and improving relationship management capability*	**Stage 8 – Exit Strategy:** *developing and maintaining an effective strategy for disengagement when necessary, incorporating a transition plan for ensuring business continuity and customer support*

Figure 8.3   Simplified relationship management compared to BS 11000, Collaborative Business Relationships

More often than not, a firm discovers that over a period a series of transactional deals have grown into a close relationship that needs a different way of working. In these cases, the choice to commence a collaborative relationship is made by default. It will then be necessary to adopt the principles and practices of collaborative management – ERM.

The beginning and end phases are comparatively infrequent events because collaborative relationships are usually relatively long-lived. Most readers will have existing collaborative relationships that are currently the centre of their focus and in need of better management. Nevertheless, within and across these phases, collaboration will build gradually as an evolutionary process, strongly depending on trust, which strengthens incrementally as successes are achieved.

The Enterprise Relationship Management Plan

At the heart of all good management processes is sound, reliable information that is formalised and available to all those who need it to perform their roles. A lack of timely, accurate information is the main source of uncertainty and distrust. The idea of a relationship management plan that helps an organisation to keep track of the activities that support a business relationship is not a new one. It may go by a number of names, including Alliance Project Plan, and Partnering Plan. We use the term Enterprise Relationship Management Plan (ERMP). It provides the support structure for framework contracting and relational governance to work together to manage the relationship.

The ERMP acts as the information focus for each collaborative relationship. It is constantly being maintained and updated. It contains static information such as the objectives, contract/agreement(s), organisational and management arrangements and contact details, and dynamic information such as changes to contract schedules, regularly updated plans, performance and continuous improvement records, minutes of management meetings including decisions, and copies of communications such as newsletters. These are summarised below:

- **Organisational arrangements:**
    - who's who, and what they do;
    - contact details.

- **Business case:**
  - high- and low-level objectives;
  - value proposition for all parties.

- **Asset register of resources and capabilities:**
  - what we all bring to the table.

- **Risk assessment:**
  - keeping an eye out for the unexpected.

- **Commercial agreement:**
  - flexible framework contracting;
  - tuned to the evolving business objectives.

- **Management activities:**
  - operations and processes;
  - managing impacts on/of supply chain stakeholders and partners;
  - performance measurement, targets and records.

- **Continuous improvement and innovation:**
  - problem-solving activity, process improvement, policy change, training;
  - management of innovation in order to build on success.

- **Knowledge management:**
  - how intellectual property is developed and shared;
  - finding and exploiting new opportunities.

- **Communications:**
  - key information such as plans, people and achievements;
  - establish an appropriate pattern of 'listening' and 'telling';
  - use all appropriate media types;
  - communicate the impact of the alliance to stakeholders.

- **Exit arrangements:**
  - consult pre-nuptials;
  - the detailed plan to unwind the joint endeavour;
  - involve key stakeholders and customers;
  - learning from experience.

The ERMP should be appropriate to the size, value, complexity and importance of the relationship. In the case of the strategic relationships between major organisations where there are subsidiary project-style relationships – either singly or in groups – there will need to be a joined-up, cascaded structure. Where an SME has a close relationship with another, the plan might exist as a very simple, one-dimensional set of documentation. However it is configured, the ERMP must be simple, clear and available to all those who need to access it for both reference and to maintain the records of activity. It can be housed in a sophisticated computer network, available on a website, in paper filing cabinets or even as a single page in an SME's cardboard folder – whatever is right for the situation.

The Relationship Managers

In each partner organisation there should be a senior executive with both strategic and operational oversight who is responsible for relationship management. In the smallest organisations, the role may well be an additional task of the owner or CEO. In very large organisations, there may be a specific department for alliance management led by a director. The relationship manager will be responsible for developing, implementing and then maintaining the collaborative business relationship management process throughout the organisation, and becomes the repository for knowledge and experience in collaborative working (see Figure 8.4). Externally, the relationship manager manages the relationships with networks of organisations, often involving dependencies – for example, key suppliers.

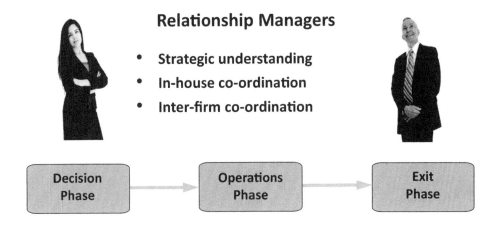

Figure 8.4   The relationship managers

The relationship manager's responsibilities are outlined as follows:

- **Senior management:**
  - Appoint experienced, knowledgeable, high-integrity staff.
  - Give the relationship manager function strategic status.
  - Keep relationship managers in post for reasonable periods, to gain experience, expertise and provide continuity.

- **Decision Phase:**
  - Use the relationship managers' advice to draft the framework contract that focuses on joint outputs and outcomes, not on the small print.
  - Define the objectives for the partnership, including the value proposition.
  - Identify opportunities and target areas that the partnership could exploit.
  - Assess risks and operational impacts.
  - Quantify the benefits.
  - Prepare a plan to exploit the selected opportunities, including costs and timescales, individual roles and responsibilities, key skills, and whether training or recruitment will be needed to acquire them.

- **Operations Phase:**
  - Maintain and manage the relationship from day to day.
  - Relationship managers co-ordinate the parent company functions that service the relationships.
  - Relationship managers jointly chair the main relationship management meetings.
  - Relationship managers measure and monitor relationship performance.
  - Relationship managers hold those responsible to account for their actions.

- **Exit Phase:**
  - Manage the exit plan.

STRATEGIC

The relationship manager needs to be aware of strategic decisions that could lead to selecting and defining the commercial arrangements for working with a new partner. The relationship manager must bring to the strategic decision-making process both policy issues for resolution and information from current partners that could allow emerging opportunities from collaboration to be exploited. This will also include the continued viability of the relationship. It is especially important to continuously reconcile and align the goals that drive alliance performance. Decisions from this process will be recorded in the ERMP.

IN-HOUSE CO-ORDINATION

The relationship manager will be responsible for co-ordinating the activities of the day-to-day operations of the organisation in order to ensure that they line up with the requirements for supporting external partners. This is important because different parts of the business will often have different priorities which may clash with the priorities for serving the end customer. The relationship manager must maintain an overview of all the activities (projects, contracts, work streams) being carried out by the organisation in order to satisfy external relationships and communicate information to all functions involved. The relationship manager must ensure that the right numbers of appropriate, trained people are in place and that they are adequately briefed. The relationship manager must mediate where conflicts occur, and ensure that decisions are implemented and documented in the ERMP.

PARTNER CO-ORDINATION

Relationship managers will synchronise work with their opposite numbers in partner companies. In some relationships, joint resources, including staff and facilities, will be provided. An appropriate level of authority is essential to enable this to happen. This is good governance involving consistent management, cohesive policies, guidance, process oversight and leadership. There need to be regular meetings to discuss past performance, current issues, forecasts and plans. Actions must be agreed, resourced and monitored, and the staff assigned must be held to account for their area of responsibility. Important elements from this activity will be recorded in the ERMP. The overall aim must be to maintain the relevance of the joint enterprise in line with objectives and against a background of changes in the external environment. When the relationship comes to an end, the relationship managers will work together to facilitate an orderly exit.

COMMUNICATE, COLLABORATE, LEAD AND SERVE

The relationship manager must have leadership qualities and the ability to communicate effectively at all levels within the organisation to maintain awareness of its important relationships and to ensure the free flow of information necessary for effective partnership working. The relationship manager must have a broad view of the business and the wider industry, and must have established effective networks. It is desirable that relationship managers remain in post for a reasonable period so that they can accumulate experience and knowledge in this highly complex role. A company that gains the reputation for successful relationship management will attract quality partners and staff. Moreover, external stakeholders such as financiers and customers will look more favourably on the firm. The relationship manager has a critical role in achieving this.

Conclusions

In this chapter we discussed the principles that underpin collaborative success. We clarified the key ideas that surround a hitherto murky area. With this new point of view in mind, the reader can now focus on using these concepts to manage key business relationships to greater advantage. You can move forward in confidence with your partners knowing that they are watching your back and you are watching theirs!

Here is a summary of the guiding principles for effective relationship management:

- **Business as usual** – Relationship management is an integral part of your business, and should not be seen as a 'bolt-on'.

- **Focus on the objectives** – Decide with your partners the value you wish to achieve from your collaborative relationships. Invest in the people, processes and infrastructure necessary, and measure your performance objectively.

- **Review what you do** – Jointly identify the things you and your partners need to do, both individually and together, to improve the way the relationships works.

- **Talk to your partners** – Develop a communication structure for working together, and maintain it.

- **Implement and document** – Jointly start doing what you agreed, and keep records.

- **Manage the ongoing relationship** – Use the ERM framework to bring together contract management and relational governance within enterprise relationship management.

- **Continuous improvement** – Make performance improvement inevitable by actively fostering the 'spark' that generates the enthusiasm to innovate and go the extra mile.

The next chapter concentrates on the practical aspects of enterprise relationship management, providing a 'how to' guide.

Chapter 9
Practical Collaboration Management: A Formal Discipline

Introduction

The Nobel Prize winning economist Oliver Williamson (1975) said that consideration of costs and risks would predispose a company to either carry out the work in-house or seek the product or service from the market – the make or buy decision. He also suggested that halfway between the two options there was a hybrid situation which he called 'relational governance'. This can involve straightforward customer–supplier manufacturing, service or project relationships, but more often these involve complex supply, co-manufacture, co-marketing, co-development and outsourcing relationships. Usually they are of a high value and/or strategic in nature.

In the previous chapter we described a formal management framework, the Enterprise Relationship Management Plan, which supports three phases of activity covering the life of a typical business-to-business relationship. In this chapter we provide practical guidance for the Decision, Operations and Exit Phases.

The Decision Phase

Choosing a collaboration partner is not straightforward, and considerations such as capability, costs and risks will only be a part of the equation. Selecting a marriage partner is not just about looks, prospects and domestic capabilities. Compatibility and chemistry are equally important. If your company is free-spirited, creative and unstructured and your prospective partner is bureaucratic and rule-bound, you will hardly be likely to develop innovative ideas quickly and take them to new markets. Does a supplier have useful knowledge? Does he have a leading position in its market? Is the supplier an innovator? Could the product be developed to suit anticipated future requirements? If any of these are true, you could be looking at a future collaborative partner, and this bears on the decision to select the particular supplier.

It is also important to consider carefully the type of contract you draft, especially if the outputs are to some extent unknown and dependent on R&D, market conditions and other external factors such as teaming up with a partner to create a portfolio of capabilities that can be harnessed into joint bids for business opportunities. Both partners need to be involved in the drafting, and a loose framework is likely the most productive arrangement.

The Decision Phase covers the following points:

- If this is to be a collaborative relationship:
  - gather the right skills and knowledge;
  - record all major decisions;
  - define your objectives.

- Shortlist likely partners, considering:
  - complementary capabilities;
  - reputation;
  - market strength;
  - culture;
  - reconcile objectives with likely partners.

- Choose partner(s), considering:
  - price and performance;
  - culture;
  - attitude to relationship management;
  - risks.

- Draft a framework contract.

- Draft exit arrangements.

- Learn from experience.

Initial Organisation Arrangements

A relationship manager must be appointed to manage the project following the criteria set out above. Individuals must be identified who will be involved in the activities to select a partner. If appropriate, they will need to be trained. Their roles and responsibilities must be defined, bearing in mind that some of them will continue to be involved in the joint enterprise in the longer term. These arrangements need to be documented in the ERMP.

OBJECTIVES

The aims of entering into a collaborative relationship, including the value proposition, will need to be broader than those for a transactional relationship because they will be strategic in nature, focusing on joint value creation, and will evolve and change over time. For example, possible objectives could be to access a new market, to benefit from partner know-how, to develop new products and services and to respond more effectively to external factors. It is crucial that a company considering a collaborative relationship establishes the objective(s) clearly at the outset, because they will determine the way the partners work together. It is possible that these objectives will only be high-level statements of intent which will crystallise into greater detail when a partner is selected and the relationship develops. It must be recognised that they will need to be reconciled with those of the selected partner(s).

SCAN THE MARKET FOR POTENTIAL PARTNERS

> *I started out delivering parcels locally. I teamed up with partners who took my business international.*[1]
>
> *(CEO SME Logistics Company)*

It is likely that the potential partners will already be known, because the field will not be large and those companies capable of meeting your strategic objectives will be even fewer. Factors to be considered include known capabilities, reputation, market strength and culture. Any nominations should be balanced against internal strengths and weaknesses, focusing on finding complementary skills, resources and capabilities. A common problem with partner selection is that companies fail to be objective in their assessment of potential partners and what can reasonably be expected of them. Like choosing a human partner, you may want to strike up a relationship with the most successful, pretty or athletic person in the room, but they may not share your enthusiasm or interest! You would be better off looking at your sources of value and competitive advantage

---

1   All the quotations interpersed with the text of this chapter are responses from participants in the authors' research.

elsewhere, in companies that have a similar interest and are willing to become interdependent for success.

> *It's not about liking each other, it's about respect for each other's capabilities.*
>
> (Chief Engineer Blue Chip Construction Company)

The desired resources and capabilities might include, for example: 'They could supply the manufacturing capacity, and we could supply the know-how.' It will be helpful to record these criteria in the ERMP in the form of an asset register. These will later be changed to 'actuals' when a partner is selected. Copies of this should be produced for each potential partner and used to support the selection.

It must be recognised that to achieve a successful collaboration, it may be necessary to share confidential plans and ideas with potential partners in order to select the right one. These initial negotiations will need to be covered by a non-disclosure agreement. Given the high degree of mutuality that is desired in a collaborative relationship, you are likely to have to convince a prospective partner to join forces.

RECONCILING OBJECTIVES

Aligned objectives are the key to collaborative relationship success. For example, one partner might want to develop new capability, whereas the other might be looking to expand into new markets. The result must be coherent, joint objectives for the relationship that encompass the differing individual needs of the partners, such as: 'We are hoping to develop a new product that will satisfy a new market.' If it is clear that this reconciliation cannot be achieved, then there is no point in going forward. The objectives of the partners need to be recorded in the ERMP.

PRICE AND PERFORMANCE

The concepts of price and performance are not as clear-cut as might be expected. Cost control and operational reliability are critical, and the capability to deliver must be part of the decision to select the partner(s). A collaborative relationship is designed to build something that neither partner could do alone, and involves a degree of innovation and the unknown. An understanding of the potential capability to work together to meet joint objectives is more important than hard evidence of past achievements. However, despite these considerations, it is still essential to have an understanding of the desired outcomes of the collaboration and their value. These may include potential revenue targets and other benefits such as gaining skills and knowledge. The evaluation should include an appraisal of how the potential value can be realised taking into consideration costs versus benefits, opportunities and risks, and resources and capabilities. A balanced appraisal of the hard and soft judgements should be recorded in the ERMP.

MATCHING CULTURE

Collaborative relationships are necessarily close. Simply linking the business process will not ensure success if the way business is carried out by the partner organisations are not compatible. For example, where one organisation is centralised, product-focused and bureaucratic and the other is decentralised, flexible and market-focused, it may be difficult to find common ground that will enable both to work together without friction. Here are some questions to ask:

- Are their commercial people willing to be flexible – do they use framework contracts which accept the inevitability of change, or are they tied up in detailed service level agreements and penalty clauses?

- Do they expect to manage the relationship through account managers who mainly focus on the next sale?

- It is important to understand the ethos and mindset of a potential partner and envisage whether or not culture matching could take place, and therefore whether collaboration would be successful. Are you prepared to work within the constraints of your and your partner's culture? Observations on culture could be added to the ERMP.

> *They are the most frustrating organisation to deal with. Everything has to be referred up the line. But their customer service is second to none and benefits us enormously.*
> *(Head of Procurement, UK Defence, Integrated Project Team)*

ATTITUDE TO RELATIONSHIP MANAGEMENT

Companies traditionally manage using standard methods such as management plans, project plans, financial statements, quality management, contract management, supplier management and balanced scorecards. Whereas these will continue to be necessary in operations and financial management, they do not measure relationship performance. Organisations need to recognise that collaborative relationships are complex and require specific management practices which will be essentially joint in nature. It is therefore advisable to seek partners that have a cohesive view of how to manage joint enterprises and have a track record of success as a result. This should be considered as a selection criterion in the ERMP.

RISKS

The assessment of risk in a potential collaborative relationship is not simple because of the increased depth and closeness it implies. Risk needs to be considered on two levels: the overall risk associated with achieving the business objective, and the risk associated with each potential partner. There is never enough time and opportunity to fully examine the detailed operation and management of a potential partner, but this does not excuse a lack of a due diligence appraisal. The risk appraisal must as far as possible take into consideration 'softer' areas as potential sources of friction that may incur additional management costs.

A potential partner's view of risk may not be the same as your own. Matters such as attitudes to investment, sustainable and ethical practices, capability to deliver reliably and the balance of power will all have a bearing. The key question is: 'Can we do business with them?' Some cultural differences may be so subtle that they are not recognised as a problem until some time into the relationship. For example, their senior management may be strongly orientated towards collaboration, but some middle management may see this as a threat to their freedom of action and obstruct new initiatives.

When you have shortlisted potential partners, it will be necessary to evaluate the identified risks with them. Risk assessment should be revisited regularly and documented in the ERMP.

COMMERCIAL CONSIDERATIONS

Successful relationships need the right mix of stability and flexibility. They require a base of rules and procedures that reflect obligations and expectations, yet at the same time there must be mechanisms to support change and reflect shifting internal and external conditions.

I'm not sure if our success in setting up a good partnering arrangement
was all luck (people) – maybe the clarity of contract aims helped.
(Project Director, Global Power Engineering Company)

The way contracts and partnering agreements are negotiated is key to ensuring both parties get what they want, and sets the tone for the relationship going forward. An agreement based on small print and/or terms and conditions backed up by stringent penalty clauses is unlikely to engender collaborative behaviours because it suggests lack of trust. The negotiations should be pitched at the right level to focus on outputs, outcomes, the benefits and the longer-term stability of the relationship rather than the short-term opportunities.

Now that we have a partnering arrangement around a good framework
contract we just concentrate on the customer – we no longer refer to the
small print.
(Senior Engineering Manager, UK Royal Air Force)

It is very important to get the commercial criteria right – not too tight, not too loose. Initially, the commercial criteria should be included in the ERMP as an aid to partner selection. A copy of the final commercial agreement or a summary should be included after partner selection.

EXIT ARRANGEMENTS

A standard aspect of the terms and conditions will be the need to end the relationship due to non-compliance. It is also entirely appropriate to plan for the natural conclusion of the relationship due to completion of the project, satisfaction of objectives or changes in the marketplace. Consideration should be given to the impact on both organisations and their stakeholders and future collaboration. Partners should develop an exit management plan before the contract is signed. This should be held in the ERMP and updated regularly. The relationship will be complex, and exit will require considerable planning and effort. Significant intellectual property rights will often be involved, as well as those investments that have been made and used by the partners. The impact on the up-stream and down-stream members of the supply chain should not be forgotten. Drafting an exit plan may seem to be a bit of a dampener on the 'marriage' celebrations, but when the relationship inevitably comes to an end, it will ensure you part as friends and all stakeholders such as customers and suppliers will be looked after.

DECISION PHASE REVIEW

Finally, at the end of the Decision Phase, it is important to review the process to understand what went well and what did not, and to ensure that these lessons are learned for the future. You will have selected a partner, but in the process you should also have made contacts with other organisations. The ERMP you raised for each should not be discarded because there is potential for future relationships with them.

The Operations Phase

The Operations Phase is all about the mechanics of managing a collaborative relationship throughout its productive life to ensure that it is efficient, effective and that there is continuous performance improvement. In practice, many of these relationships often evolve from long-term transactional dealings where trust and familiarity are already established. In such cases, the establishment of collaborative working practices will require managers to observe the principles of collaborative management described in Chapter 8 and put in place the ERMP framework covered in the Decision Phase.

GOVERNANCE

The arrangements by which collaborating organisations manage their joint enterprise will involve both individual and joint structures, as shown in Figure 9.1.

Because of the difficulties associated with co-ordinating cross-boundary operations, governance processes must be very clearly specified and will be dependent upon high-level agreement. Governance will vary depending upon the characteristics of the relationship.

Senior managers will agree responsibilities, organisational arrangements, resourcing, funding and performance targets, both internally and jointly. Training may be necessary. The relationship managers will co-ordinate activities within their own organisations and jointly. Care should be taken to ensure that the right balance is struck between formality and informality. Too much formality will stifle innovation and involve bureaucracy. Too little control will result in costly underachievement, despite the enthusiasm this gives rise to. These arrangements will be documented in the ERMP. The example of a framework in Figure 9.1 shows how the partners link up to work together and to manage the enterprise.

Figure 9.1   Joint management during the Operations Phase

Note how joint objectives, key performance indicators and organisational arrangements set by the relationship managers govern the relationship's operations. Note also how senior management have a key role in overseeing the strategic direction, including looking for new opportunities to extend the collaboration.

Regular senior management meetings should take place between the partner organisations in order to review past and present performance, to ensure that the joint objectives are still appropriate, and finally to look ahead to how the joint business will develop in the next period. The relationship managers will play a key role at these meetings.

The relationship managers are responsible for operational oversight of their organisation's collaborative relationships. They will work very closely with their opposite number(s) in the partner organisation(s). As set out above, they focus on meeting joint objectives and performance indicators utilising the joint organisation. The significance of the role is that it not only manages the routine, but it also instigates activities that make continuous improvement happen and provides the ability to exploit new opportunities the joint business opens up. The effectiveness of the collaboration will be increased by ensuring that individuals or teams take on relationship responsibilities which span both organisations. These will cover areas such as operational processes, risk, resourcing and performance.

REGULAR OPERATIONAL MEETINGS

Managing the action is the bread-and-butter role of the relationship managers. In our research, we have discovered that over 75 per cent of relationships do not do this. 'Why?' we ask, to receive the answer, 'Because the consideration of this detail might sour the relationship.' It is thus no wonder that many so-called collaborative relationships fail to live up to their expectations, and it can be inferred that many are neither happy nor productive. At the very least, a monthly formal operational meeting chaired jointly by the relationship managers must take place. They must clearly minute these meetings, hold people to account for their actions, and record all decisions and results in the ERMP. Progress must also be communicated and celebrated. As a minimum, the agenda should cover the following items:

- Review performance targets in last period and issue statistics.

- Review work/orders in progress.

- Review forecasted work, sales and orders in next period.

- Consider and solve problems.

- Actively seek out and initiate process improvements.

- Review future plans (including new products) and initiate preparation.

- Review industry and technology updates.

- Identify policy issues to refer to senior management.

- Involve other supply chain partners.

PERFORMANCE MANAGEMENT

In organisations, we measure everything in order to understand performance now and how we hope it will turn out. Understanding the performance drivers of a collaborative relationship is essential because there will be a series of hard and soft measures that cross the boundaries of the firms. Given the often strategic importance and value of the joint enterprise, it is obvious that the relationship managers and their senior management know exactly what is going on and where the trends are leading. Failure to understand crucial pointers buried deep in the complex interactions between organisations will lead to the insidious growth of distrust and the eventual failure of the relationship.

Expectations need to be tempered with realism. Flexibility, trust and forbearance are essential, as is constructive problem-resolution. For example, in an R&D situation there may be many false starts before the final design is achieved. The solution is a joint proactive governance arrangement where all the parties have the same overview of performance and its management. In this way, there are no surprises and issues should not escalate to the point where the contract penalties or exit clauses are invoked.

> *The secret of success is small, easily controllable work packages and teams, where greater onus is put on individual responsibility and where performance is clearly visible.*
> *(Head of Product Development, Global Snack Foods Manufacturer)*

As shown in Figure 9.2, effective performance measurement underpins ERM. It is important to create a clear joint understanding of those aspects of the joint business that affect the bottom line and the ability to create value. Traditional quantitative measurements such as balance sheets and sales figures, while necessary, focus on internal, historic performance and largely ignore the process dynamics that cross company boundaries. Dependence on these alone often leads to poor co-ordination at the interfaces, and results in problems that take you by surprise. Difficulty in understanding what is going on leads to symptoms being treated, rather than the causes. By the time the failures emerge, they are serious and relationship-threatening.

> *At times, we are more concerned with metrics than real achievement i.e. we spend a lot of time 'weighing the pig' rather than feeding it!*
> *(Director of Major Projects, UK Government Department)*

Prevention lies in uncovering and then addressing the drivers of poor quality, lack of communication, inability to deliver on time and so on. In addition to the standard measures of time, cost and quality, what is needed is a means of going beyond the existing measures of performance.

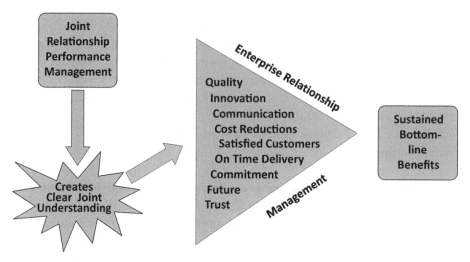

*The process for co-ordinating all the business activities essential
to joint success*

Figure 9.2   How relationship performance management contributes to
business success

This must take into account the impact of environments, markets, products, IT, functions and processes. It must especially include the behaviour of customers and suppliers, outsourcing partners and the like, as well as the people within the organisation.

Implementing a performance measurement system that is optimised specifically for relationship management enables the following key performance drivers to be measured and understood across the joint enterprise:

- **innovation** – the 'leap of faith', being creative, flexible and resilient;

- **investment** – alignment of objectives, investment in people, know-how, infrastructure and management effort, and long-term vision;

- **communication** – open and transparent, frequent and extensive learning, planning and anticipating;

- **operational effectiveness** – focus on service and product delivery, lower joint costs and risks, building trust;

- **value** – joint relationship success, perceived and actual benefits, overall satisfaction.

In addition, it is important that these measurements provide a view of the softer aspects – the key attitudinal gauges – of a relationship, such as trust, commitment and long-term orientation, that have a motivational impact on operational performance. Figure 9.3 shows an example traffic light report demonstrating how these key performance indicators can be portrayed in a simple and readily understandable format.

The report was created from a survey involving the knowledgeable people in each organisation, and the figures and colours (here shown as shades of grey) represent levels of satisfaction. We have already described in a previous chapter how the red (dark shading), yellow (light shading), yellow/green (light grey) and green (grey) traffic lights together with the percentage satisfaction scores show the strengths of managers' feelings. By comparing and contrasting the responses, it is possible to see quite clearly where the strengths and weaknesses lie and where there are opportunities to improve performance. If more than two partners were involved in the collaborative enterprise, such as in a consortium or in a supply chain network, there would be an additional column of traffic lights for each party. Regular relationship performance measurements allow the relationship managers to precisely target remedial effort, set business objectives and monitor progress over time.

> *Personal trust helps us to face each other over performance issues in a business-like, joint problem-solving way.*
> *(Supply Chain Manager, Food Manufacturer)*

Whatever approach is adopted, it must not be onerous to apply, it must be trusted by all parties as a non-partisan perspective, and it must be acted upon jointly. Lastly, it must be integrated with the joint governance system that is put into place to manage the relationship and must be documented in the ERMP.

> *The traffic lights were very interesting and revealing. I am concerned about the parts where our views are at odds. We are going to re-look at how we are doing business together with our partner and will use these differences to get things started.*
> *(Head of UK Air Refuelling Tanker Aircraft Integrated Project Team)*

Performance at a Glance

- **Innovation:** the leap of faith, being creative, flexible and resilient.
- **Investment:** Alignment of objectives, investment in people, know-how, infrastructure and management effort, and long-term vision.
- **Communication:** open and transparent, frequent and extensive, learning, planning and anticipating.
- **Operations:** focusing on service and product delivery, lowering joint costs and risks, building trust.
- **Value:** perceived and actual benefits, satisfaction.
- **Long-term Orientation:** encouraging stability, continuity, predictability and long-term joint gains.
- **Interdependence:** loss of autonomy is compensated through the expected gains.
- **C3 Behaviour:** Collaboration, Co-operation, Co-ordination, joint resourcing to achieve effective operations.
- **Trust:** richer interaction between parties to create goodwill and the incentive to go the extra mile.
- **Commitment:** the relationship is so important that it warrants maximum effort to maintain it.
- **Adaptaion:** willingness to adapt products, procedures, inventory, management, attitudes, values and goals to the needs of the relationship.
- **Personal Relationships:** generating trust and openness through personal interaction.

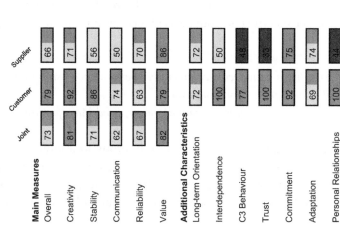

Main Measures

	Joint	Customer	Supplier
Overall	73	79	66
Creativity	81	92	71
Stability	71	86	56
Communication	62	74	50
Reliability	67	63	70
Value	82	79	86

Additional Characteristics

Long-term Orientation	72		72
Interdependence	100		50
C3 Behaviour	77		48
Trust	100		33
Commitment	92		75
Adaptation	69		74
Personal Relationships	100		44

Bandings	Colour	Response
0-49%	Red	Urgent Action Required
50-59%	Amber	Corrective Action Required
60-74%	Amber/Green	Corrective Action Recommended
75-100%	Green	Ok Unless High Priority

Figure 9.3   Measuring collaborative relationship performance

COMMERCIAL CONSIDERATIONS

Some relationships are based on informal 'handshake' agreements. Others will be governed by formal arrangements such as written contracts. Whichever is in place, ERM will provide a structure within which collaborating partners can develop workable commercial arrangements including objective performance targets, open-book transparency and incentives. Just reviewing the contract at set intervals is unlikely to enhance the performance of a collaborative relationship which is subject to change and flexibility. The commercial managers need to be included in the relationship managers' meeting so that they will be aware of developments and be able to maintain the currency of the contract, agreement or service level agreement. This continuous review process reduces the cost of commercial management, and more importantly, reduces the risk of contract breakdown and associated relationship disruption. The updates should be reflected in the ERMP.

CONTINUOUS IMPROVEMENT AND INNOVATION

From performance measurement and joint operations will emerge the need to do things differently and better. Collaborative working is about creating an atmosphere that stimulates innovation. It will give rise to proposed improvements, which should be formally evaluated, and if agreed, adopted as change initiatives. One approach might be to have a joint improvement process, which would:

- have a cross-functional view;

- track ideas;

- identify potential benefits;

- prioritise initiatives;

- establish joint roles and responsibilities for implementation.

This process will be jointly managed by the relationship managers and documented in the ERMP.

> *They are a small innovative company who can turn out two or three new products per year. We can only do something like one product every three years.*
> *(Director of Innovation, Global Food Products Manufacturer)*

KNOWLEDGE MANAGEMENT

When two or more partners collaborate, they will contribute specialised knowledge to the enterprise. Examples are product designs, sales leads, R&D results, market research and margins. If there is confidence that this knowledge will not be misused (for example, used without the permission of the owner), then the quality and quantity of that contribution will be greater. In these circumstances, an important product of the alliance will be new knowledge, both joint and individual, which can be exploited profitably in a self-reinforcing cycle. The relationship managers will need to be aware of their organisational policies on the sharing of intellectual property, and must expect to act as brokers between their senior managers and the relationships they manage. A flexible approach is needed, because the generation of knowledge and the need to exploit it, both internally and jointly, will be an ongoing feature of collaboration. There needs to be a regularly reviewed, jointly agreed policy statement in the ERMP that outlines how knowledge will be managed.

COMMUNICATIONS

Collaborative relationships draw upon people with relevant skills and knowledge from the partnering organisations, therefore there is an increased need to use communication to establish a sense of teamwork and common purpose. There is also a need to ensure that processes both within and between the partner organisations integrate. Those involved need to know not only where they fit, but also how their processes interact with others both inside and outside of their company. They will also need to know what progress has been made, what current developments are taking place, and what is planned. Personal and team accomplishments will need to be celebrated. Outside the relationship team, both companies will need to be kept informed, and in the wider environment, individual and joint 'press releases' will need to be planned and issued if appropriate. The relationship managers must establish the lines of communication and ensure that information flows are effective. There needs to be a defined communication process and plan incorporating formal and informal communications, such as briefings, newsletters, intranets, social media, and shared working environments, which should be documented in the ERMP.

> The fact that we do not have an effective performance measurement system whilst our partner believes we have is a real failure to communicate.
>
> (Director of Customer Service, Defence Manufacturer)

BEHAVIOUR: RELATIONAL GOVERNANCE

Collaborative relationships are inevitably deep and long-lasting, and will evolve over time. Although the contract will provide the foundation for the relationship, continuous discussion and negotiation at all levels will allow innovative ideas to be captured, included in the ERMP and implemented. Managing the joint enterprise as a team is the most effective way of getting the balance between formal and informal processes right. This is the ability to work together across organisation boundaries to create the value that the individual partners could not create separately. Therefore, a different style of behaviour is needed to generate the best outcomes.

Some relationships have a formal behaviour charter launched with a fanfare of trumpets and reinforced by regular team-building events. For others, it will just be business as usual. However it is done, the premium is on participative leadership rather than the traditional, directive style of management. It will be necessary to create a working environment where all feel that they can contribute freely and trust their colleagues and organisation to go the extra mile. Continuity, predictability and long-term joint gains are also valued. It should be noted that trust between people and organisations will only build up over time as a result of an accumulation of small teamwork successes.

BUSINESS CONTINUITY PLANNING

Because of the close linkages between collaborating partners, supply chain disruption effects on the joint enterprise are likely to be more serious. Analysis of potential risks and maintenance of contingency plans need to extend beyond the relationship to encompass the important members of the supply chain. This, together with necessary modifications to the exit plan, should be documented in the ERMP.

THE EXIT PHASE

All relationships, including alliances, partnerships, joint ventures, supply chains and those between customers and suppliers, come to an end one way or another. There are likely to be two different situations where the relationship is no longer needed:

- **Mutual agreement** – This may arise where, for example, the requirement for the product or service declines or ceases to exist because of market conditions or agreed time limit, as in the case of a completed project or a change in regulatory or other external conditions.

- **Non-performance** – This may arise as a result of action on one side or the other that triggers the break-up of the relationship. For example, culture mismatch could become serious enough to make an exit necessary, as could a failure of effective enterprise relationship management or underperformance. Alternatively, it could arise where one or other of the partners ceases trading, is taken over and/or cannot fulfil its contractual obligations.

If the management of the relationship has been conducted effectively, then distrust, acrimony and divorce will be avoided. The prime objective of the Exit Phase is an orderly, amicable dissolution where all parties get their fair share and customers are not disrupted. The exit plan was originally drafted at the start of the relationship, lodged in the ERMP and adjusted to take account of changes throughout its life. It can be seen as the inverse of the processes and activities that created and developed the relationship. In a recent high-profile contended relationship termination, a High Court judge took IBM and AstraZeneca to task for not having an exit plan.

Finally, the exit plan gives the parties the opportunity to reflect on their performance throughout the collaboration and to learn from experience. Those organisations that excel at collaborating are not only more successful, but their enhanced reputation draws higher-quality partners into their fold, and stakeholders such as investment sources are more likely to support them.

EXIT STRATEGY

Because the relationship has been collaborative, the exit is likely to be complex and require considerable planning and effort. As noted earlier, considerations include any intellectual property rights and investments such as skills, materials and infrastructure, as well as the impact on the up-stream and down-stream members of the supply chain. If at all possible, the exit should be managed so that the impact on both organisations and their stakeholders is minimised and the prospects of future collaboration between the partners is not jeopardised.

Because of their knowledge and operational experience, the relationship managers will have an important role to play in managing the exit process.

The ERMP will provide the starting point because it holds a comprehensive overview of the relationship, its objectives and it operations and well as the draft exit plan. A checklist of actions is presented below:

- Relationship managers appoint teams with the requisite skills and experience, including commercial, operations, sales and other experts.

- Update the ERMP exit arrangements and draw up a project plan.

- Agree how the intellectual property rights and assets will be allocated.

- Agree business continuity actions with supply chain members and stakeholders.

- Review and agree all contractual terms, including any variations.

- Implement the plan.

- Jointly review and record the lessons learned at the time of closing the ERMP. These need to be fed back into the respective organisations so that benefits can be realised in future projects.

Conclusions

As in any aspect of business, you must only do what is necessary to improve performance of your particular collaborative relationships, but this must be built into your standard operating procedures. To do it effectively requires dedicated resources, in particular specialist relationship managers whose role is to co-ordinate the outputs of their organisations to satisfy the needs of the collaborative enterprise as well as to co-ordinate operations with the partner organisations. It is thus clear that most importantly, Enterprise relationship management is all about joint activity and achievements.

Chapter 10
A Strategic View –
The G + H Partnering Types

Introduction

Successful partnerships constantly strive to maintain the forward momentum implied by the Partnering Behaviour Success Spiral. They do this by generating value as a consequence of the way in which the partners are innovative, manage the relationship within agreed standards of behaviour, and create and capture value through a focus on synergy and critical, positive self-evaluation. The two models we have described will allow you to gauge the overall performance of a partnership or alliance rather than the more customary and much more limited financial view. These models provides a framework in which the seemingly random variations in the behaviour of partners can be consistently interpreted and understood, whether their relationships are supply chain partnerships, key accounts, marketing channels or strategic alliances. Next, we will go a stage further and describe a more strategic approach, the Gibbs + Humphries Partnering Types, and show how it provides another perspective for understanding important alliances and to drive change programmes. It allows characteristic relationship types to be identified based on proven parameters, and critically, offers clear pointers to managers on the best way ahead.

The Gibbs + Humphries Partnering Types

When viewing a very large number of partnerships using our six super-factors – Collaborative Innovation, Partnership Quality and Value, matched to ratings of success or failure – we noticed that some clear patterns emerged. It appeared that the vast majority of relationships fell into one of eight groupings or partnership types, and on closer inspection, each type had a distinct, individual character which could be characterised. This led us to an appreciation of the performance and management challenges that faced the partners in each type. Moreover, on this basis, we gave each of the G + H Partnering Types a name to reflect its personality and main behaviour tendencies. It also led us to the realisation that if you can categorise the type of partnership in which you find yourself, you are in a much better position to apply the correct management actions to achieve your objectives. Figure 10.1 shows how the super-factor values generate the eight G + H types.

The Partnering Types are as follows:

1.   **Evangelists** – appear as a marriage made in heaven and are usually good collaborators, but may be prone to rest on their laurels.

2.   **Stable Pragmatists** – tend to be in a tough business, but recognise that they are in the same boat and soldier on doggedly, sometimes for many years.

3.   **Rebellious Teenagers** – almost your worst nightmare; a great partnership, but challenging, annoying and marked by very heated discussions.

4.   **Evolving Pessimists** – continually focus on what is not working rather than what is working well; they have good intentions and struggle doggedly against the odds, but effective service delivery is some way off.

5.   **Captive Sharks** – partnership hostages who work together because they have to; usually proactively aggressive.

6.   **Cherry Pickers** – just in it for the money and the short term, despite appearing at times to be committed.

7.   **No Can Dos** – the businesses are simply pulling in opposite directions with no common ground; a history of bad behaviours and outcomes has poisoned the atmosphere.

8.   **Deserters** – this stage typically precedes dissolution of the partnership, or litigation.

EVANGELISTS

Evangelists are characterised by their above-average assessment of all aspects of the partnership.

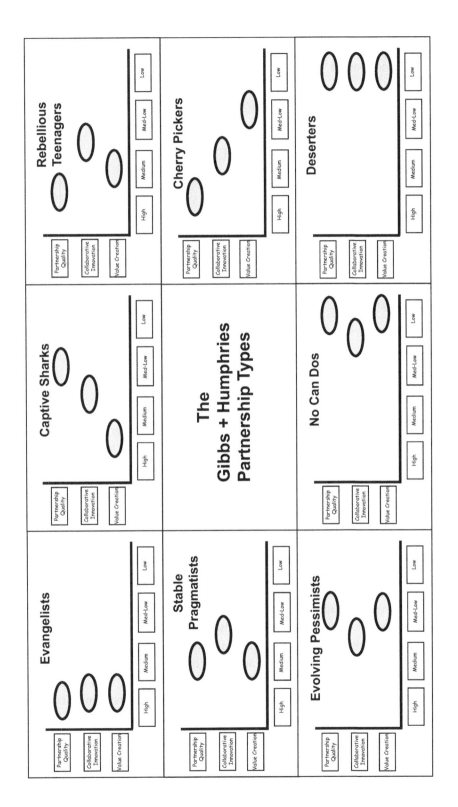

Figure 10.1   Relational exchange super-factors generate eight G + H Partnering Types

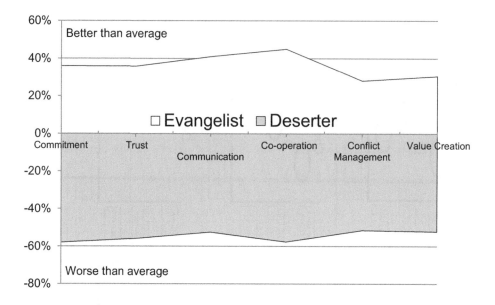

Figure 10.2   Comparing Evangelists with Deserters

Figure 10.2 shows the performance of Evangelists and Deserters based on the average of approximately 10,000 partnerships that have been assessed.

The assessment is broken down into six major dimensions which determine the quality (Trust and Commitment), collaborative capacity (Communication and Co-operation) and business efficiency (Conflict Management and Value Creation) of a partnership.

Evangelists can form a well-established platform for the development of a market. They are exceptionally loyal, and will spread very positive messages about the host firm. Typically, in a multi-level partnership or channel, we will see very high levels of end customer satisfaction where Evangelists are acting as intermediaries. They are often present during the early or late stages of a market's development. In the initial stage of a typical product or market life cycle, they can take on the role of early adopters, being willing to take products and services which are less than refined and fault-free. They will do this in the understanding that they believe fervently in the goals and ambitions of the firm. During the more mature phase, they will continue to be a consistent partner, placing great emphasis on the product, service or initiative even in the light of a declining business.

Evangelists can also be very effective collaborators, going out of their way to support and drive the initiative forward. The result can be efficient, effective supply chains focused on customer requirements.

The downside of Evangelists is that we rarely find them representing significant business opportunities, either in scale or return on investment. The expectation is that given the assessment of the partnership, this should be the partnership type displaying the greatest returns; however, the harmonious conditions mean that the necessary 'heat' needed for a truly effective partnership is missing. This means that creative innovation can falter as the boundaries of the partnership tend not to be pushed too wide. Having said that, inter-organisational learning can sometimes thrive in this sort of situation, where partners are very willing to exchange knowledge and intellectual property within the safety of a well-established relationship.

There is an argument that suggests that the host firm in an Evangelistic partnership is investing too much in the relationship and would benefit financially from reducing the level of investment without impairing the level of mindshare. One major downside is that Evangelists can be very resistant to change. Sometimes, when change does take place it will lead them to becoming very easily disenchanted with the partnership and transforming into a Deserter. Alternatively, their resistance to change, especially if there are a large number of similarly minded partners in a marketing channel, for instance, can significantly impair a firm's ability to drive through critical initiatives and respond to competitive pressures; professional services firms can be particularly prone to this challenge.

In terms of Evangelists, the host firm needs to make a judgement on whether it is about doing less, not more – less direct investment, less communication and less joint planning might still produce exactly the same performance, but at a lower cost. The risk is obviously that as a host firm reduces its commitment to the partnership, the Evangelist is eventually likely to respond negatively. Alternatively, the host firm might decide that the very special relationship that it has with the Evangelist can be better leveraged or driven harder, so that the full relational rents from the partnership can be harvested. For example, they may be chosen to act as reference point for other potential partners or alliances.

Managing Evangelists can, on the one hand, be very easy, and yet on the other, very frustrating, as they can often seem intractable in their ways. It is a very fine line between reaping the benefits from the relationship, and looking for innovation and change that could disrupt the partnership. The level of interpersonal trust can be high, and this can create very tight bonds (social and commercial) between the organisations involved. A change in personnel in terms of account manager can therefore have a significant impact on the business

Like any change management project, successfully initiating a new policy or strategy with an Evangelist requires the Evangelist to recognise the need for change in the first place, and to recognise that this change will strengthen and deepen the partnership and its common aims, rather than create something new and foreign.

Managing Evangelists can require directional management rather than the collegiate style which is probably already in place. Being directional runs the risk of upsetting the partner, but may be the only route to persuade them to change and become more dynamic and responsive to market or policy changes.

The level of operational satisfaction of Evangelists is particularly high. Their evaluation of the critical marketing elements of Communication, Competitiveness, Brand, Profitability and Support are all in the upper quartile, and likely to be a near perfect score. Therefore, their feedback on new programmes or collateral can be particularly revealing.

DESERTERS

Deserters are characterised by their well below-average assessment of all aspects of the partnership.

It is important to recognise the exceptionally low score on all aspects of the partnership. There are simply no redeeming qualities in the host firm or the relationship itself.

Deserters will be present at any time during a market or partnership life cycle. The belief that a Deserter will only emerge towards the end of a life cycle is naive and incorrect. The cause of their dissatisfaction can sometimes be located in a single area, whether a policy change or a specific action by the host firm that has been seen negatively, but generally their assessment is the result of a culmination of factors. Typically, we will see low levels of trust and commitment emerging, and a fall-off in the extent to which the partner buys into the mission and philosophy of the partnership itself. Collaboration decreases, and the confidence the firm has in the underlying value proposition evaporates. The Deserter is hanging onto to the relationship, but has already mentally moved on; as a result, switch selling or other opportunistic behaviour is taking place.

As a consequence of the above, it would be a misjudgement for a firm to think that promotional or other exceptional investment will change the Deserter's mindset. Two strategies can be explored in managing this particular partnership type. On the one side, the firm can take the initiative and simply terminate the partnership, minimising further costs and efforts in maintaining an ineffective partnership. Sometimes, however, a Deserter can represent a major opportunity, and it is probably worthwhile trying to re-construct the partnership. In this situation, it is important that trust is re-established in the partnership: this can be trust in the sense of a firm doing what it said it was going to do, trust through displaying competence and ability, or trust in showing empathy about the partner's predicament and responding benevolently.

The level of interpersonal trust in a Deserter partnership is very low. It can be too simplistic to consider that changing the account or alliance manager will immediately remedy the situation, but this is a course of action that can be explored (if the commercial value and opportunity warrants it). In some instances, changing the account manager can be successfully combined with appointing a partnership 'godfather' – a very senior figure within the host firm who takes a decisive role in supporting the revival of the relationship by addressing concerns on a very direct basis with the appropriate resources to support their delivery. This enables the account manager to get to grips with the development of the business without being overburdened by day-to-day issues and legacy queries.

One characteristic of Deserters is their very low assessment of the operational performance of the firm. In many instances, this is unwarranted, and is a consequence of other partnering difficulties such as a lack of trust and credibility. However, it can be worthwhile exploring issues with the partner, as this might identify genuine weaknesses and threats that could be latent concerns for other partners.

Deserters' assessment and responsiveness to most marketing tactics is very low. They have in many instances tipped beyond the point where such activities are valued. However, firms should consider revitalising the commercial foundations of the partnership, reaffirming the strength of the brand, demonstrating the competitiveness of the offering, and ensuring that the business model fits.

Typically, the re-construction of a Deserter is very similar to the recruitment of a new partner: trust needs to be established, the economic proposition re-explored, the processes and policies agreed, and so on. The main difficulty lies in overcoming the antipathy that has been created, and the first step to this is open and honest dialogue.

There is no consistent period during which a partnership resides in the Deserter space. These relationships can terminate quickly, stagger on for a length of time, or in some instances simply change backwards and forwards between No Can Dos and Deserters. The knowledge of what type of space your partnership occupies gives the manager the ability to align tactics and resources appropriately. In the case of Deserters, the manager has stark choices to make about whether or not any further action is appropriate.

STABLE PRAGMATISTS

Stable Pragmatists are characterised by their above-average assessment of all aspects of the partnership (see Figure 10.3). If there is a desired state in terms of partnering, then this is most closely represented by this type. This is not to suggest that such relationships are perfectly harmonious, but that they produce the desired results of an effective and efficient partnership.

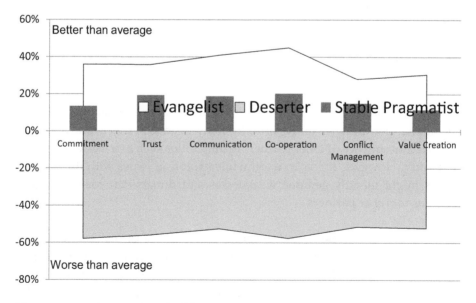

Figure 10.3   Comparing Stable Pragmatists with Evangelists and Deserters

The Stable Pragmatist displays world-class assessments, but falls short of displaying signs of diminishing or negative returns as seen in the Evangelist.

Stable Pragmatists can be most welcome during the early phase of a market or product life cycle, although typically they are more likely to be present when the relationship has achieved a degree of stability but nevertheless remains in growth. Successful relationships are characterised by the degree of investment leverage, inter-organisational learning and governance. In the Stable Pragmatist, assets are being leveraged, but there is significantly more investment that could be made subject to the willingness and ability of management to development the necessary business cases. Inter-organisational learning can take place because effective communication is already present, but the processes are not as tightly aligned as they could be and some further improvements can be made. All of this adds up to a very significant opportunity for professional alliance or partnership managers. They are blessed with a partnership that is performing well, but remains capable of enjoying further continued growth.

Continued performance improvement is possible, and this is driven by effective management – the leadership style, whether directional, participative or consultative, is immaterial. More important is the ability of the alliance or partnership manager to draw on the appropriate internal resources and chains of command to get things done. In many instances, particularly in strategic alliances, the success of Stable Pragmatist partnerships is very heavily dependent upon the political power and position of their alliance managers.

The nature of this type of partnership means that it remains in a state of tension (not necessarily conflict), which means that issues continually need to be addressed. One aspect that will require frequent discussion and reiteration is the business model itself – the extent to which value or profit is achieved and captured by both parties. The questioning of the profitability of the partnership can lead to significant opportunities for process improvement, to the benefit of all stakeholders and customers. Therefore, the judicious use of process metrics to review performance and uncover inefficiencies is important. It is equally important that these metrics are not used as a tool for recrimination or punitive measures – such behaviour would seriously impair the partnership's performance.

The overall improvement of the partnership can be addressed by developing a greater appreciation and understanding of the partner's motivation and critical success factors. This improvement in open dialogue will support the improvement of joint planning. In this sense, joint planning is associated directly with better communication, better co-ordination of activities and a realistic appreciation of alternative business models.

Stable Pragmatists have a relatively positive assessment of the host firm's brand and reputation. In many instances, firms will generally exaggerate the relative importance of their brand in negotiations and discussions. Therefore, while the Stable Pragmatist does not hold a negative view, the host firm should not assume that its brand positioning and strength is without question, and should actively inform and educate the partner on the broader (networking and eco-system) benefits of working with it.

REBELLIOUS TEENAGER

Rebellious Teenagers are probably the most complicated of relationship type, as they are full of conflicting dynamics and behaviours and are very difficult to manage well (see Figure 10.4). Rebellious Teenagers are not unusual, and typically represent significant commercial value for the host firm.

It is important to recognise the relatively poor low score on Conflict Management, despite the above-average commitment and acceptable levels of trust.

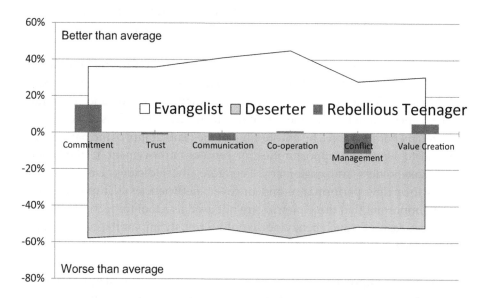

Figure 10.4   Comparing   Rebellious   Teenagers   with   Deserters   and Evangelists

The Rebellious Teenager type of relationship will typically occur prior to a market or product maturing in a life cycle pattern, and can often be the saviour of a firm's partnering initiative as it goes into decline.

To Rebellious Teenagers, the relationship itself can be very important. They feel they have a stake in making the partnership work, but by the same token feel that the partnership might be going in directions different from those they originally signed up to. Conflict is likely to be very high, and this is not made any easier by the fact that Rebellious Teenagers do not communicate very well. They are as reluctant to share their concerns as they are to hear the messages and information provided by the host firm. The host firm is seen as inflexible and inconsistent, and liable to make promises that it does not keep, often using threats to get the partner to toe the line.

The management of Rebellious Teenagers is very difficult, but the scale and value of their business can make it worthwhile. Due to the typical maturity of the relationship, important personal bonds will have been established with Rebellious Teenagers, and these can be used to draw out the issues the partner has, and create an opportunity for the goals and ambitions of the collaboration to be re-stated and reaffirmed.

The effective management of Rebellious Teenagers concentrates on setting and agreeing common goals and targets, then ensuring that they focus their attention and resources on achieving these goals. This is easier said than done, because of the poor and difficult communication processes that are associated with this type of partnership. The polite veneer or loud disagreement of the partner makes it difficult to ascertain exactly what it is aiming for, and therefore can cause significant frustration for the account manager. A purposeful starting point for an account manager dealing with a Rebellious Teenager is to try to uncover the nature of the underlying grievances, and in particular why it feels that the host firm does not have (or no longer has) its best interests at heart. The cause of this disaffection can sometimes be found in strategic changes the host firm is undertaking. In marketing channels, this might be about setting up a new partner, or in strategic alliances it might be an acquisition or policy change. By their nature, these tend to be matters which are beyond the scope of the alliance or partnership manager to change or nullify. As a result, the partnership manager needs to drill deeper to communicate the aims of the strategic change more effectively, and then to drill down into the detail to understand how the change will directly impact the partner. It is at this more granular level that some (token) adjustments or benevolent actions can be undertaken.

Rebellious Teenagers will typically migrate in one of two directions. Successful management will see them becoming Stable Pragmatists, with a realistic sense of proportion about the partnership and complementary increases in effectiveness and efficiency. Alternatively, they can transition into Captive Sharks, resentful of what was once a positive relationship, and now holding on simply because they need to.

CAPTIVE SHARKS

Captive Sharks are characterised by their well below-average assessment of virtually all aspects of the partnership (see Figure 10.5). The one area in which they tend to score high is commitment.

It is important to recognise the relatively high score on Commitment and Value Creation. The Captive Shark is tied to the partner for economic and possibly contractual reasons, but all other attributes of the partnership are seriously impaired.

Like many partner types, Captive Sharks can be present at any time during a market or partnership life cycle. However, they are most commonly present during the top end of the development phase and as a market is in decline.

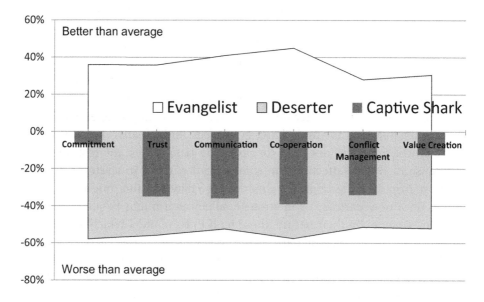

Figure 10.5   Comparing Captive Sharks with Evangelists and Deserters

During the early phases of a relationship, these partners can often be Evangelists who have invested heavily in the product or market or alliance, but as things develop, their evangelism tends to become resentment as they count the cost of early over-investment. Similarly, during the decline period, Captive Sharks will hang on in there – and it is here that we see their true colours as they appear increasingly to be hostages of the partnership. Finally, Captive Sharks can also emerge as a consequence of contractual or other commercial obligations. They can remain with a partner because the contract forces them to do so, because a customer's client necessitates it, or because market conditions dictate that they should.

Working with Captive Sharks is very difficult. Their assessment of virtually all collaboration initiatives will not be flattering. However, financially these partners can be a firm's largest or most profitable. Recognising that they remain committed to the partnership means that they will continue to invest time and effort in ensuring that every ounce of benefit is realised. While they are not averse to some opportunistic behaviour, their commitment means that they are unlikely to want to jeopardise the partnership, so any misdemeanours will be slight.

Managing Captive Sharks requires a firm and steady hand. Discussions will not be easy, and will often be heated, but consistent behaviour and extreme responsiveness and agility will mean that Captive Sharks can be managed without too much disruption to the business. Critically, Captive Sharks can be a great resource for understanding the motivation and business models of your partners, and through this learning, adapting processes and programmes to meet their needs. Therefore, while some Captive Sharks will descend to become Deserters, they can often be transitioned into Rebellious Teenagers or Stable Pragmatists.

CHERRY PICKERS

Cherry Pickers are characterised by their average assessment of virtually all aspects of the partnership (see Figure 10.6). The one area in which they tend to score high is Conflict Management. In this respect, Conflict Management illustrates the general *laissez-faire* attitude to the partnership.

It is important to recognise the exceptionally low score on Co-operation. In many instances, the lack of co-operation is a fundamental aspect of Cherry Pickers.

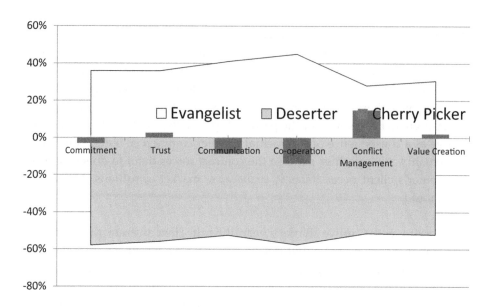

Figure 10.6   Comparing Cherry Pickers with Evangelists and Deserters

Cherry Pickers are pervasive. They will turn up in many partnering relationships, and it is their opportunistic nature that makes them the first to join a party, and often the first to jump ship. They are insidious, and it is often difficult to separate genuine commitment from their relatively shallow appreciation of the partnership. Cherry Pickers are self-satisfying. They see benefits in the relationship simply from the functional capabilities of the product or service, and little at all from working with the firm that provides them. They will be reluctant to co-operate, as this implies some form of commitment and a perception of additional effort in their part.

Nevertheless, Cherry Pickers can be very important in driving the volume and scale of operations. They will get behind an initiative or relationship and work hard at making it a success. For this reason, they are important players in many strategic networks and channels. They can also represent great potential opportunities, and it is for this reason that firms need to make sure that they evaluate the relationship carefully. Investing in Cherry Pickers will have little impact on their behaviour; they will simply take short-term advantage.

The day-to-day management of Cherry Pickers is relatively pain-free, if frustrating. They do not challenge the partnership, will fully leverage and understand the firm's processes (particularly support and escalation processes), and will be generally supportive. Partnership managers need to beware that they are not taken in by this acquiescence, as Cherry Pickers will often quit the partnership very quickly and move on to the next low-hanging fruit. To fully exploit opportunities, the host firm needs to move Cherry Pickers out of their current type and into another, ideally a Stable Pragmatist. To accomplish this, Cherry Pickers need to be managed carefully to improve their perception of the credibility of the host firm and the prospective gains from greater engagement; this can be as simple as cross-selling and up-selling, or it can be more complicated and take longer, as in the case of service provision and R&D alliances.

Cherry Pickers have a positive appreciation of the strength of the host firm's brand. This appreciation can be leveraged by encouraging the partner to become more aligned and integrated with the brand through accreditation and certification programmes, co-branding initiatives and cross-licensing. These activities will increase the partner's commitment and investment in the partnership. Once this deeper engagement is established, then creating opportunities for collaborative and co-operative activities should follow.

EVOLVING PESSIMIST

Evolving Pessimists evaluate a partnership as just short of acceptable (see Figure 10.7). Their response on a series of attributes is consistently low. There are few upsides, but equally, nothing is yet seen as desperately failing. In fact, one of the key characteristics of Evolving Pessimists is that they attempting to improve conditions and make an initiative more effective and efficient.

Evolving Pessimists are less committed to a partnership, but maintain a reasonable assessment of the level of communication and co-operation that takes place.

Evolving Pessimists will typically emerge relatively late in the market or partnership life cycle. They are cynical about the likelihood that the partnership will be successful, yet they see that the opportunity for success exists. Therefore, they can frequently be turned around by effective management and dutiful investment. The downside is that they do not represent a high-return partnership. This lack of profitability or productivity becomes habit-forming, and the partners find it difficult to break the mould. While blatantly adversarial behaviour might not be prevalent, there are nevertheless significant criticisms on both sides of the performance of the other partner.

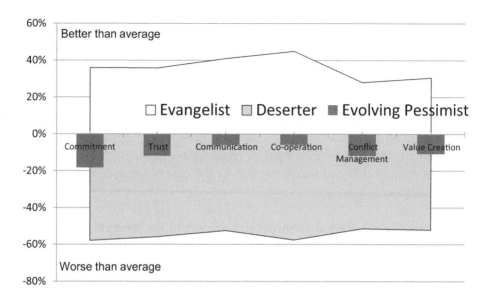

Figure 10.7   Comparing Evolving Pessimists with Evangelists and Deserters

A critical success factor for developing Evolving Pessimists is driving C3 Behaviour, which is all about Collaboration, Co-operation and Communication. Evolving Pessimists lack effective joint planning and efficient operationalisation of these plans to the extent that these are serious hindrances to the revitalisation of the partnership. C3 Behaviour is closely associated not only with communication, but also trust, and in this respect the host firm needs to signal to the partner its credibility, steadfastness and consistent support of the programme or project. This will then create the platform for partnership development.

The management of Evolving Pessimists requires patience, as it can sometimes take protracted effort to turn them around. However, it is not uncommon for an Evolving Pessimist to migrate to a Stable Pragmatist, with all the associated commercial benefits. A consultative or participative management style is generally more effective, as the issues need to be brought to the surface, reviewed, discussed and corrective actions agreed.

Evolving Pessimists are likely to assess the degree and extent of sales co-operation at an average level – neither impressed nor strongly dissatisfied. This therefore represents an open door against which the host firm should push and encourage further joint selling activity. Critical in this instance is the extent to which the host firm responds to the requests and demands of the partner, who will not see the host as reliable or flexible. It is also important that in any joint planning, the host firm builds a very good understanding of the business model and objectives of the partner; Evolving Pessimists see only a weak alignment of common goals and mutuality of interest with their partners, which can impede effective joint planning.

NO CAN DOS

No Can Dos have a generally low assessment of most aspects of the partnership (see Figure 10.8). They are very similar in this respect to Deserters, but their distinguishing feature is that while they remain relatively upbeat about the some of the interpersonal aspects of the partnership, they are also likely to flare up in terms of conflict and dissent. This translates into a partnership that lacks drive, vision and energy, which will get translated into low assessment of ease of doing business and other general operational failings.

It is important to recognise the exceptionally low scores on most areas, in particular Commitment, yet their assessment of Conflict Management is reasonable, just short of what could be considered average.

No Can Do partnerships can often be found in the toughest of economic conditions. Heightened uncertainty, stiff competition and semi-monopolistic conditions have created an inward focus of the partnership; the consequential focus on process, service levels and contractual obligations is based on a paradigm that less than optimal performance is to be expected. This can force the account manager to become bound up in the micro-management of all aspects of the partnership, with a resulting lack of market- or customer-directed collaboration and co-operation. This view of the world is systemic, and can easily become culturally embedded.

All of this translates into a less than effective and efficient partnership. Returns on investment are not optimal, and there is often a proliferation of human resources and decision-making structures (committees and sub-committees) which hamper the partnership's ability to respond to opportunities.

For these reasons, managing No Can Dos requires tough and often bold and sweeping decisions to be made. The relationship continues, based on an expectation of failure, but is maintained on the basis that there are few alternatives. This resignation to fate, with all its negative connotations, can often be the consequence of several years of poor operational behaviour coupled with limited alternative suppliers or partners.

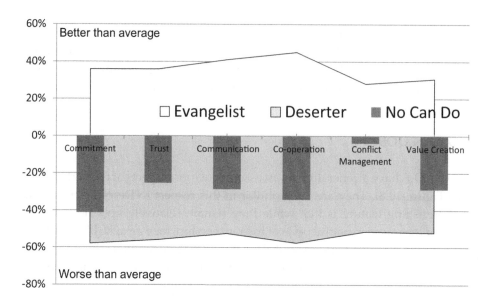

Figure 10.8   Comparing No Can Dos with Evangelists and Deserters

One remedy is to break out from this cycle by forcing change upon the incumbents. This change can be created externally, and often occurs in political, economic, social or technology areas (PEST). No Can Do partnerships are especially prevalent in highly uncertain, complex environments, and an open and honest appraisal of the market and industry conditions (and their consequences) can be a spur to initiating change. A focus on the external world must be coupled with internal assessments of critical processes and programmes so that improvements in quality and efficiency are highlighted. Alternatively, change can be brought about through organisational and financial structural changes, such as the creation of a joint venture. These are major decisions, so they are dependent upon the importance of the commercial value generated or transacted by the partnership. Changing the governance structure of a partnership can sometimes be an effective last-ditch tactic for rescuing the business, especially in monopolistic or semi-monopolistic conditions.

No Can Dos are very unreceptive to most elements of the marketing mix. Neither communication, product nor brand address their concerns and expectations. In this instance, trust can begin to be rebuilt in the relationship by undertaking an assessment or audit of marketing flows, identifying critical areas of weakness and responding accordingly. This review of operational activities can act as a signal (especially if supported by investment) to the partner that the relationship might have some value and attractiveness.

Conclusions

The Gibbs + Humphries Partnership Types provide a unique insight and perspective on managing inter-organisational relationships. The findings show that partnerships of whatever type – whether outsourcing arrangements, marketing partnerships or supply chain collaborations – can be defined and characterised with reference to six super-factors. These variables then enable the definition of nine partnering types. The vast majority of partnerships fall into one of these Gibbs + Humphries Types. This means that it is possible for a relationship or partnership manager to classify and categorise the partnership and to understand the factors and drivers that are shaping the nature of the collaboration. This simplification does not negate the complexity of the task, but does potentially make it more comprehensible.

A further key point is that partnerships are not immutable. They can and do change over time. While few Deserters can be pulled back from the brink without considerable effort, Evangelists can easily slide into a No Can Do state. These changes can take place over a reasonably short period, so that an Evolving Pessimist can turn into a Captive Shark within a few months. This means that it is possible for the efforts of a relationship manager to improve the performance of a partnership to be rewarded within a quarter or two. The notion that any change in a relationship is glacial in speed and hard won is not supported by experience or evidence.

Chapter 11

ERM – the Core Competence of the Future

Introduction

This book has begun where many books on relationship management in alliances and partnerships have ended. We have described how the trend for businesses in all sectors has been towards increased diversity through networks and outsourcing. The result has been an ever-growing challenge for managers dealing with the exponential increase in strategic cultural and operational complexity. We have discussed strategic responses and examined in detail the management and understanding of relationship performance. We are able to do this because our research and practical experience enable us to say that we are experts in the field. In this final chapter, we propose that enterprise relationship management should become the critical company core competence of the future.

Markets and Organisations

Globalisation and the Internet are changing the world we live in at an enormous rate. The emergence of new markets in the Far East and South America – many at the 'industrial revolution' stage with all the consequent problems of boom, pollution and regulatory free-for-all – are dominating the near horizon. The dilemma for Western countries is how to bridge the cultural divides and take advantage of these new opportunities without excessive exposure to fearsome risks. In the face of so much cheap production capacity, many have seen a resurgence of innovation generated by groups of partners. As a result, they have made substantial inroads into the high-end luxury goods markets serving the developing countries' growing elites.

The networked economy is rewriting traditional business thinking about ownership and creating alternative business models based on interdependent and complementary alliances, partnerships and consortia. Delivering value consistently and building new-style relationships with well-informed customers who see e-commerce as a commoditised marketplace pose enormous challenges. In response, firms are using the communication speed and accuracy of the Internet to involve increasing numbers of very small organisations to provide a responsive, reliable service to their end customers.

As well as these key features, increasing consumer knowledge and choice are forcing organisations to address their sustainability and ethical dimensions and to adopt responsibilities that in the past would not have featured in their business models.

The shape and pace of today's global market has prompted some commentators to propose that any competitive advantage will now be fleeting and transient. The speed of change, information exchange and fewer barriers mean that holding onto any advantage will in itself require a new set of skills.

The advantages themselves have also moved on from cost advantage, functional differentiation and segmentation. In the future, firms will have to consider personal engagement with their customers, who are looking to satisfy a host of sophisticated requirements. Customers will seek fulfilment, not just in the product itself, but also in the transaction and consumption experience, how the product is acquired, and how it is used. For instance, music is now downloaded from the cloud, possibly not locally stored nor owned, and enjoyed when, how and where the listener wants.

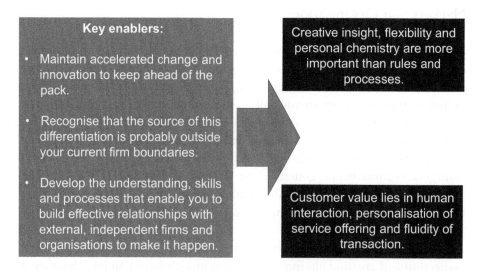

Figure 11.1   Enablers and sources of competitive advantage in 2017

The challenge this places on individual organisations is such that the chances of ongoing disruptive and creative innovation coming from within the company's own walls is remote. Inter-organisational innovation becomes a prerequisite.

In this tumult, one underpinning factor will remain as a constant core company competency: the ability to maintain effective relationships (see Figure 11.1).

Collaboration: Up Close and Personal

Traditional command and control management systems saw organisations as independent entities that jealously guarded their freedom of action. In particular, they kept their relationships with other firms at arm's length. Moreover, they maintained a strict focus on cost, quality and time, expecting to keep control by means of pedantically drafted contracts. A spate of partnering failures over the years has shown that effective relationship management within collaborative partnerships is the crucial ingredient to achieve success. It requires a number of very different competences, such as flexibility, trust, commitment, forbearance and transparent communications, to be deployed. In scenarios such as IT outsourcing and facilities management, the customer often has the supplier located within its own organisation's buildings, so close-quarters teamwork is key.

It is thus the pooling of collective capabilities that enables alliances to deliver value to the partners and their customers by:

- reducing time to market;

- reducing joint costs;

- enhancing opportunities;

- reducing risk;

- improving risk;

- optimising resources;

- increasing customer satisfaction and confidence;

- achieving superior returns that could not be achieved by the partners individually.

Partnering Governance

The tension between relationship management and contracting has increased as dispersed and fragmented organisational structures have become more prevalent. It is clear to us that these two must be reconciled within ERM.

Traditional management theory on contracts states that partnering governance has to deal with three main challenges:

1.   safeguarding exclusive investments;

2.   measuring relationship performance;

3.   adapting to unforeseeable changes.

Thus, companies have often relied on contract terms and conditions to manage suppliers. However, collaborative relationships are complex, strategic in nature, and their outcomes are difficult to predict. In these circumstances, writing comprehensive, enforceable contracts is extremely difficult, and presents a significant challenge.

The Governance Challenges

Exclusive investments are the specialised human and/or physical resources each party contributes to the relationship. For example, an information systems supplier will have to provide a customised service to the client. Similarly, the client will have to develop an understanding of the supplier's procedures, approach and language to make effective use of its service. Both parties may thus become locked into the relationship. This dependence on each other requires management effort to maintain positive outcomes and to avoid the friction that can arise from feelings of claustrophobia.

As mentioned in Chapter 9, in a highly publicised case on the acrimonious dissolution of their relationship, a High Court judge criticised IBM and AstraZeneca for failing to have an exit plan which ensured the equitable distribution of intellectual property rights.

Performance measurement can be used to link relationship rewards to productivity, which allows the partners to share the value they create fairly. It is thus important to build a clear joint understanding of those aspects of the relationship that affect the bottom line and the ability to create value. In addition to those measures of gain share, criteria such as levels of partnership effectiveness should be included. When there is a lack of transparency, trust diminishes, as does commitment. Friction costs will eat away at profits.

> *Their mentality is to make the most money from us and there is very little of working as a partnership towards a common goal, sharing objectives and risks.*
> *(CEO SME Manufacturer of Specialist Chocolate Products)*[1]

Uncertainty challenges the partners to adapt to problems raised by unforeseeable events. For example, in the external environment, rapidly changing technology is a dominant feature. Adaptation requires a high degree of C3 Behaviour (Co-ordination, Co-operation and Collaboration) by relationship partners. These behaviours require significant management effort and are critical to relationship survival.

> *The benefit of our partnering arrangement is we are 'future-proofed', uncertainty is removed, we can plan and we can really focus on the customer.*
> *(Head of Production, SME Fashion Clothing Accessories Manufacturer)*

Contract Management

Formal contracts represent promises or obligations to perform particular actions in the future. They specify the actions required and conditions of contractual breach, and also a framework for resolving disputes. These three challenges, singly or in combination, make effective contracting difficult to achieve. They also stretch the ability of the relationship to adapt. The 2008 terrorist attack in Mumbai caused a number of companies to rethink their overseas sourcing strategies. The recent shift to total service contracts in facilities management requires a completely different approach to performance measurement. The temptation is therefore to write more complex contracts containing clauses to cope with every eventuality, but inevitably they will always be incomplete.

---

1   All the quotations interpersed with the text of this chapter are responses from participants in the authors' research.

This leads to high costs, both upfront and ongoing. For example, clauses may specify third-party monitoring, disclosure of necessary records to justify work done, and if possible, the use of benchmarks to gauge the performance of the work done.

A global food manufacturer outsourced some seasonal product lines to a small, world-class, niche producer. The supplier was expected to fill retailers' shelves with high-quality, low-cost items. However, the customer insisted on controlling raw material sourcing and demanding weekly production statistics as if it was one of its own factories. The result was severe friction between the partners and disagreement over the performance of third-party logistics providers.

Thus, formal contracts of this type impair the efficiency of strategic, collaborative relationships. Furthermore, they can signal distrust of your partner and encourage rather than discourage opportunistic behaviour such as actively looking for loopholes in the small print and finding ways to minimise the profit you have to share.

Some have said that contracts are not appropriate for collaborative relationships, where a hand-shake should suffice. However, there is still a critical need for contracts to provide a legal structure to support the joint enterprise. However, they must shift from merely specifying deliverables to providing frameworks that facilitate the evolution of highly co-operative, flexible relationships that are focused on outcomes – relational contracting. An example in common use is the NEC3 ECC Form of Contract used in engineering, construction and other sectors: 'Where traditional forms of contract can promote an adversarial relationship between contractor and client, the NEC promotes a partnering, collaborative approach which has a consistent record of delivering projects on time and on budget at its core.'[2]

---

2   'NEC3 Contracts', NEC: https://www.neccontract.com/Products/Contracts (accessed 14 January 2014).

A pair of successful SMEs had grown their businesses together over twenty years without a contract in place. However, difficulties in creating and launching a new product made them realise that their processes, communications and technical co-ordination had become disjointed. The lack of a clear framework for managing the relationship resulted in higher process costs, communication disconnects, loss of competitive edge, and growing hostility.

The process of sitting down together to agree on value goals, operational tactics, the relationship management structure and performance measurement will promote collaborative working. Moreover, it will ensure that the relationship is flexible and constantly able to maximise its potential.

Relational Governance

There is some confusion about what collaboration between outsourcing organisations actually means and looks like. Traditional business relationship management approaches to working with customers and suppliers often ignore the essential 'jointness' implied by collaboration. In our view, collaboration is where firms enter into buyer–seller relationships, supply chain partnerships, services provision or any other alliance combinations. They work *together* using their specialised resources innovatively to achieve aims and objectives that they could not realise on their own at an acceptable cost.

Collaborative relationships are based on the meeting of minds. Joint relational governance emerges from the values and agreed processes found in social relationships, which may be more effective at minimising the effects of the challenges than detailed contracts. These are usually scattered across any number of roles and individuals who are working to achieve local outcomes, such as the salesman who is keen to keep the customer happy so he can land the follow-on deal.

Relational governance promotes positive attitudes resulting in:

- **flexibility** – the ability to adapt in a fluid environment;

- **solidarity** – encouraging joint problem-solving and creating a commitment to joint action through negotiation;

- **information-sharing** – encouraging transparency, short- and long-term planning, and joint goal-setting.

Subsequently, this commitment leads on to C3 Behaviour.

Two food supply chain relationship managers got on really well. Both had a complete grasp of their organisations and their operations. They had worked through their firms' goals and developed a workable plan to achieve value for both organisations. Their attitudes and professionalism permeated the entire relationship. They not only trusted each other, but also respected each other's capabilities to the extent that they were able to form a successful united front when dealing with their end customer, a major supermarket retailer.

Relational governance fosters expectations of continuity. It encourages the partners to take a long-term view of the relationship, including investments, performance, innovation and rewards. Over time, trust will develop and strengthen. Under these conditions, working together is likely to bring about increased interdependence, where the parties become reliant on each other to achieve their goals. The growth of trust ensures that neither feels constrained by the loss of autonomy.

> We need to create a more open environment of trust where either party
> can raise an issue which gets actioned.
> *(Head of Software Project, Global IT Outsourcing Company)*

However, although relational governance creates a suitable environment to overcome the governance challenges, it is unstructured and unbounded in nature. It therefore limits the effectiveness of teamwork and the performance improvement that collaboration can achieve. The provision of a formal management structure is therefore critical to collaborative relationship success, but this does not come without a cost.

Enterprise Relationship Management

The formalised ERM approach brings partnership management into sharp focus because it becomes proactive, disciplined and accountable. It is comprised of formal organisational arrangements that ensure all activities are jointly managed at all levels. It needs to be supported by an objective performance measurement system that allows creation of a clear joint understanding among the partners and enables them to get things done to time, cost and quality. Moreover, it puts in place a management system that has the ability to always create and capture the maximum joint value possible within the relationship. Its success is dependent upon the commitment of dedicated resources, but it will become a valuable capability in its own right as expertise grows in the management of complex outsourcing relationships.

> *We are starting to face up to performance issues at our regular meetings. In the past mutual defensiveness got in the way of making improvements. This has been a very hard matter to tackle but it is getting easier as we get used to working together.*
> *(Project Manager, National Construction Project).*

Some large organisations have an alliance management office staffed by professionals with a director-level head. The office is the focus of all relationship management activity. It has the clout not only to manage project relationships with partner organisations, but also to co-ordinate the activities across departments within the firm that contribute to the satisfaction of those projects. The department, with its privileged position, is able to recognise important information or capabilities arising out of collaboration and to act as a catalyst for organisational learning and the exploitation of new skills. It accumulates knowledge and expertise about the process of collaboration and change management that help to make the firm and its partners more successful at collaborative change. As a result of its growth in reputation as a team player, important stakeholders such as investors will be more enthusiastic about offering support for new enterprises and other successful companies will be keen to work together with the firm.

At the operational level, the alliance management department will directly affect the level of constructive harmony in the partnerships. This significantly reduces the management costs usually associated with firefighting and increases the levels of goodwill, which directly improve trust, innovation, communication quality and value capture. Of course, having a dedicated alliance department or even an ERM director will be beyond the means of many organisations, but the role can still be recognised as a formal secondary task for a senior individual. Given the central position within most firms of the commercial director, perhaps this is a new role for this department?

In practice, ERM is carried out operationally by relationship managers, who will typically focus on matters such as these:

- Review performance targets in last period and issue statistics.

- Review work/orders in progress.

- Review forecasted work, sales and orders in next period.

- Consider and solve problems.

- Actively seek out and initiate process improvements.

- Review future plans (including new products) and initiate preparation.

- Review industry and technology updates.

- Identify policy issues to refer to senior management.

- Involve other supply chain partners.

- Review and update the commercial agreement.

- Update the Enterprise Relationship Management Plan.

Regular meeting to discuss lead times, deliveries and technical problems are essential enablers to building trust. A key aspect of this is the management of innovation and a joint improvement process that will:

- have a cross-functional view;

- track ideas;

- identify potential benefits;

- prioritise initiatives;

- establish joint roles and responsibilities for implementation.

A supplier placed one of its electronics specialists in its customer's R&D team. By replacing a number of older components with a single module, he was able to slash production costs by 20 per cent and shortened the development time of a new product by a year. The new product had a greater range of features, was more reliable, used less power, and its potential market life was extended. The final offering proved to be competitive breakthrough in terms of technology, price and improved market share. Both firms secured 30 per cent revenue increases.

Effective Collaboration for the Future

Collaboration is where firms freely enter into relationships in order to work together using their specialised resources innovatively to achieve aims and objectives. Customers want more than efficient, cost-effective turnkey operations. They want successful, cutting-edge suppliers to contribute to the achievement of their strategic objectives. Suppliers want a deeper, more valuable, long-term relationship with successful customers. Bring these two together within an effective relationship, and it is possible to open up new opportunities to share increased returns.

The secret to doing this is to combine framework contracts and relational governance within the ERM structure, which provides the joint, formal organisational arrangements. The framework contract defines the required governance structure and the broad objectives of the relationship. It becomes a living entity that adapts to the changing needs of the joint business. It promotes stability, and thus supports the relationship's capacity to respond to challenges. Relational governance provides the essential behaviours and attitudes such as openness, honesty, trust, co-operation and long-term orientation that enable effective teamwork.

It is this combination of framework contracts and relational governance within enterprise relationship management that generates higher collaborative relationship performance than any governance mechanism in isolation. In particular, the effective collaborative will provide greater resilience in the face of the operational and commercial risks that will continue to expand in an ever-uncertain world.

Whether you have a supplier in Tianjin or 15 miles down the road,
whether you have a joint venture partner in Madrid or New York,

whether you have an OEM customer in Loughborough or Sao Paulo; an unrelenting focus on developing and maintaining mutually successful medium and long-term business partnerships through meaningful collaboration is critical to building a company in the 21st century. After all, with the complexities and competitiveness of today's business environment, none of us can do it all on our own, can we?

(Mike Reilly, CEO, Ether NDE)

Appendix 1:
Co-destiny – the Xerox and
Fuji Xerox Partnership

The goals of Xerox and Fuji Xerox can be described as mostly
compatible and partly conflicting.
(Yotaro Kobayashi, former Fuji Xerox President and CEO,
cited in Gomes-Casseres and McQuade 1991)

We have used this case study in a number of our lectures and classes. The iconic Xerox Corporation has seen many trials and tribulations over its long history, but its relationship with Fuji Xerox remains one of the most remarkable, durable and adaptive partnering examples, and offers many lessons for those wishing to utilise the full force of ERM in their alliances and partnerships.

In 1960, Xerox launched its 914 copier. In the same year, its total revenues topped $40 million. It was poised to see unprecedented growth over the coming decade, but from its US home, the company also recognised that it lacked the international coverage that would be needed to exploit the opportunity the 914 represented. A 50/50 joint venture with the UK-based Rank Organisation had already been formed. For Xerox, the single objective was to provide the much-needed sales coverage outside the domestic market; for Rank, the move represented an opportunity to diversify from its core motion film distribution business. The agreement gave the joint venture the right to manufacture and market Xerox products worldwide, excluding the United States and Canada. Rank Xerox moved quickly to establish subsidiaries across Europe and Australia, and was soon in dialogue with Japanese companies eager to conclude licensing agreements.

The Japanese market represented a significant opportunity. The fundamental complexity of the Japanese language and the large numbers of characters meant that typewriters were difficult to use, and even the smallest office needed to make copies. The then prevalent technology was the relatively cheap diazo type copier. Local manufacturers held sway, and Ricoh enjoyed a dominant 75 per cent market share. These diazo copies were unpleasant to work with, and the concept of the cleaner plain paper 914 copiers was an offering banging at an open door.

Japanese regulations at the time forbade foreign firms from importing and selling into the market. There was an upfront requirement to sell through local licensees or some form of strategic alliance, and so the courting from 27 prospective Japanese partners began. From this group, Fuji Photo Film (FPF) was selected, primarily on the strength of the personal relationship that had been built up between the respective leaders, Thomas Law at Rank Xerox and Setsutaro Kobayashi at Fuji Photo Film.

The joint company Fuji Xerox (FX) was therefore established in 1962, on a 50/50 basis, to sell in specific Pacific Rim markets and then subsequently, as a result of governmental pressure, to manufacture (albeit initially subcontracted back to FPF) Xerox copiers.

'Its small, but it's a Xerox'

Even prior to the formation of FX, Fuji Photo Film had been investing in research and development into the base technology of xerography, and once the agreement was signed, Fuji appears to have lost no time in enhancing its knowledge. Engineers were accumulating knowledge and know-how on the Xerox equipment, machines were disassembled to understand how they were put together, and by September 1962, the first Japanese-manufactured Xerox 914 was rolling out of the factory gates. Within a matter of the years, the assembling of imported components had progressed to 90 per cent of parts for the 914 being sourced from local or regional suppliers.

FX continued to invest, extending its sales coverage and marketing capabilities – by 1967 Japan was outselling France and Germany. But FX did not hold back from building its xerographic and manufacturing expertise. Various technology agreements had been put in place which enabled information-sharing to take place between Xerox (Rank Xerox had taken a step back in 1969 and the relationship was now being orchestrated by Rochester) and FX without the risk of intellectual property seeping into Fuji Photo Film.

At the same time, competitive pressures from Ricoh and the expiration of Xerox patents led to a critical turning point in the partnership. To secure the manufacturing source that was seen as critical to FX's ongoing success, Peter McColough, then Xerox CEO, persuaded FPF to transfer copier manufacturing rights to FX at the time of the opening of a purpose-built state-of-the-art manufacturing and engineering factory.

But within FX there was growing discontent with being restricted to manufacturing and marketing products designed in and for the domestic US market. FX's managing director at the time, Nobuo Shono, described their perspective:

> We had been insisting that the Xerox Group needed to develop small copiers as an integral part of its worldwide strategy. However, Xerox's attitude was that the low end of the market was not a priority ... . On the other hand, we were seeing rising demand for small copiers in Japan.

Xerox, on the other hand, not only did not see the need for such a development, but also did not seem too concerned about what was going on so far away in what was considered a relatively small market. This myopia allowed FX to give full rein to its ambitions.

In 1973, FX introduced the FX2200, a small, light and slow copier, with a cost base approximately half that of Xerox's equivalent machines and an innovation that represented a clear step in FX's corporate evolution. In Japan, it was launched with the slogan: 'It's small, but it's a Xerox.'

However, Xerox itself remained introspective, and while Rank Xerox took 25,000 units, FX products were excluded from the domestic markets. Xerox was now struggling. Its near monopoly had been eroded to the extent that by 1975, there were more than twenty plain paper copier manufacturers worldwide. Its worldwide share had fallen from 93 per cent in 1971 to 60 per cent in 1975. In 1976, Ricoh took the dominant market position in the US.

'The Japanese were selling products in the United States for what it cost us to make them. I was not sure if Xerox would make it out of the 1980s,' said David Kearns, then CEO of Xerox. Despite this, Xerox still would not respond, and indeed cancelled its own development of small and mid-range products, suggesting that FX should abandon its own low-end development projects. FX had little or no option but to continue its own development. For Kobayashi, it was a question of ensuring the ongoing profitability of FX, and he drove through the development completion and subsequent launch of the FX3500 in 1979. The FX3500 went on to break the record for annual sales of copiers in Japan. In the same year, under continued pressure from the competitive inroads being made by Japanese copier manufacturers and the absence of its own products, Xerox started to import FX products into the United States. The tide had turned.

A Stellar Partnership

If the tide had turned in 1979, continuing the metaphor, the 1980s saw some choppy water in the relationship between Xerox and FX.

Over the coming decade, FX would step up its development and manufacturing capabilities such that by the 1990s, virtually all of Xerox's entry-level products were FX based units. The relationship between the companies also changed to reflect the emergence of new roles. Technologies and licensing agreements between the companies continued to develop. In 1983, the manufacturing license fee (MLF) was introduced – a fee of up to 20 per cent which was added on the unit costs of FX copiers for assembly outside Japan as recompense for FX's investment in plant and equipment for manufacture, and crucially for the R&D it was undertaking. During the same period, the royalty payment FX had been paying Xerox reduced, reflecting the decreasing value in the base xerographic technology.

FX was also looking to expand its sales coverage. The existing agreement allowed it to sell to Xerox (and Rank Xerox) and Indonesia, South Korea, the Philippines, Taiwan and Thailand. But it remained barred from selling to the lucrative markets in Australia, New Zealand, Singapore, China, Malaysia and Hong Kong. These continued to be within the sales territory of Rank Xerox. FX argued that this not only limited its coverage and scale economies, but also meant there was a confused sales strategy in the Pacific Rim area. Rank Xerox sold at high margins, controlled from London via Hong Kong and focused on the high-end market. FX priced low, pitched low and partnered with local companies to form joint ventures.

Canon was competing aggressively in all geographic markets, and its entrance into Australia was heralded with the competitive landscape tipping to the low end, low prices that FX championed. It was also developing and marketing a range of laser printers under its own brand, as well as selling OEM versions to firms such as Hewlett-Packard. The combination of digital scanning and laser printing represented a real technological threat to Xerox and FX, and previewed the multifunctional devices that are prevalent today. There was also the first recognition of what was perceived as a serious concern. Canon, in combination with HP, could irreparably damage the companies' business strategies. With Canon coming in from the low end with its copier offerings, and HP targeting the corporate office space with laser printing in an increasingly PC-focused and networked environment, Xerox could be effectively squeezed out of existence.

Canon's perceived strength was that it was a single entity. Xerox CEO Paul Allaire summarised the general view: 'When we negotiate with Fuji Xerox, we can't just represent ourselves. We have to find what is fair and equitable to essentially three partners. Canon is 100 per cent owned by one company.'

The structure of the joint venture itself was beginning to hamper the development of the business. Xerox had moved from taking at times an arm's length, almost paternalistic, position in the relationship, through one of disinterest, to recognising that FX represented a core asset of the company. The challenge now presented was how this competency was to be leveraged.

In the late 1980s, there was a shift in the relationship. Residents soon appeared in Xerox offices worldwide, representatives of FX who were on extended tours of duty to understand more about Xerox's operating plans, developments and capabilities. These FX personnel were mirrored by Xerox staff spending time in Japan. These exchanges of people (and know-how) coincided with a more collaborative approach to R&D. Rather than FX developing and Xerox importing, or vice versa, there a number of joint projects began to emerge. FX and Xerox would take turns to adopt the lead or support role on projects.

The Co-destiny III Task Force was initiated to address directly the question of how Xerox and FX should extend and formalise the collaboration that was now recognised as offering significant competitive advantage.

Both firms saw the threat that Canon represented. They also recognised the market opportunity for laser printers. They most wanted to optimise the profit margins to be gained. At the same time, they both had their own strategies for doing so. Inevitably, these strategies were not synchronised. The consequence was that FX wanted high mark-ups on the costs, while Xerox wanted an acceptable gross margin. Negotiations on negotiations led to a plethora of pricing plans for the various products. These negotiations between the two partners burnt up high-level management time, which was time diverted from focusing externally on what the competition were up to.

The innovative solution was the creation of Xerox International Partners (XIP), established in 1991 after protracted negotiations as a joint venture between Xerox and Fuji Xerox to sell FX printer engines, digital marking engines, full-system printers and digital copiers to OEMs for resale under another manufacturer's brand name. This created a series of benefits. The potential market for Xerox was extended into the OEM sector. FX products could incorporate the printing or marking engine of a device from another firm, where the OEM had selected its own controller, in a different chassis and with a different brand name. This was a lucrative business. It also enabled manufacturing economies of scale for FX as well as fuelling incremental R&D.

There were plenty of early wins. Within a couple of years, XIP could claim that it was providing laser printer engines to a number of companies, including Compaq Computer Corporation, Digital Equipment Corporation, Genicom Corporation and SunPics (a Sun Microsystems Inc. business).

In 2004, XIP outbid Canon (still a major force, and supplying market engines for HP) to win the Dell OEM business:

> Under the agreement, Fuji Xerox will build on its strong patent portfolio, which is shared with Xerox Corporation, and manufacturing capabilities to provide world-class technology based on Dell's strategy and specifications. Dell will acquire the products through Xerox International Partners, a U.S.-based joint venture between Fuji Xerox Co. Ltd. and Xerox Corporation. XIP offers digital marking engines, including printers and other document imaging systems, for resale under other companies' brand names.
>
> Dell Chairman and CEO Michael Dell announced the technology agreement today during a presentation at the 2004 International Consumer Electronics Show.
>
> 'Dell's new relationship with Fuji Xerox and XIP provides access to a heritage of world-class technology that will fuel the continued expansion of our printing and imaging business,' said Tim Peters, vice president and general manager, Dell Imaging and Printing. 'Fuji Xerox is known for innovation and leadership and will contribute significantly to Dell's goal of providing a superior customer experience.
>
> Sunil Gupta, XIP president and chief executive officer, said the agreement will help deliver alternatives to customers and provide new revenue and market opportunities.

'This agreement will change the competitive landscape. Xerox and Fuji Xerox together hold one of the strongest and most enviable intellectual property and patent portfolios in the imaging industry,' said Gupta. 'Combining our expertise with Dell's complements Xerox's growth strategy to expand market coverage and broaden access to industry-leading imaging technology.'[1]

Conclusion

At the time of writing (March 2014), the relationship between Xerox and Fuji Xerox remains in place, a recognised asset to the corporation and an unprecedented source of technology and know-how: 'Our technology licensing agreements with Fuji Xerox ensure that the two companies retain uninterrupted access to each other's portfolio of patents, technology and products' (Xerox 2011).

Firms enter into strategic relationships for a number of different and at times overlapping reasons. Academics Doz and Hamel (1998) suggest the following six strategic logics:

1.   **building critical mass** – ensuring that a firm has the resources or mass to enter to compete in a market;

2.   **reaching new markets** – leveraging another firm's access (whether legitimate, or physical presence or reputation) to enter a market, typically overseas;

3.   **building new competences** – utilising a partner's knowledge and know-how to build new skills within the firm;

4.   **building nodal positions in coalitions** – being part of a group or consortium or companies, frequently to influence the acceptable of standards or legal requirements;

5.   **plugging skills gaps** – using the resources of the partner simply because it can do things your resources cannot;

---

1   'Xerox International Partners and Fuji Xerox Align with Dell to Expand Imaging and Printing Marketplace'. Press release, BusinessWire, 8 January: www.businesswire.com/news/home/20040108005628/en/Xerox-International-Partners-Fuji-Xerox-Align-Dell#.VAsecKO6O-k (accessed 6 September 2014).

6.   **creating new opportunities** – working with a third party to innovate and develop new products or services.

The relationship between Xerox and its joint venture partners illustrates how the rationale can evolve over time.

The Xerox/FX/Fuji Photo Film/XIP relationships reflect the sort of network or constellation that is becoming increasingly apparent as an extended organisational structure for many firms.

These clusters or constellations can form the basis for competitive advantage – not just in terms of sales and marketing, innovation and R&D, but critically in global supply chains as well, such that the English academic Professor Martin Christopher suggests that 'we no longer compete as individual companies, we compete as supply chains, you know, so it is not Ford competing with General Motors or Toyota, its Ford's supply chain competing with General Motors' or Toyota's supply chain.'[2]

---

2   Cranfield School of Management (2007) 'Interview: Professor Martin Christopher. Logistics and Supply Chain Management: Creating Value Added Networks'. Bedford: Cranfield School of Management: www.som.cranfield.ac.uk/som/dinamic-content/media/knowledgeinterchange/booksummaries/Logistics%20and%20Supply%20Chain%20Management/Transcript.pdf (accessed 21 June 2012).

Appendix 2: Dimensions, Constructs and Measures

Our research and the understanding we have gleaned through that research is founded on a set of dimensions, constructs and metrics or measures. The development of the Gibbs + Humphries Partnership Types is based on the six super-constructs that in turn are based on a series of metrics and measures that help us to understand the dynamics of partnerships. Relationship appraisal can only be undertaken if agreed and selected metrics are used. These measures have been formulated through the work of many academics, and the Bibliography reflects only the key contributors. Taken as a whole, they provide a comprehensive view of the wide range of components that make up inter-organisational relationship management. This appendix therefore details the six super-constructs along with the metrics and measures that can be applied.

Table A2.1   Relational exchange quality dimensions and constructs

Commitment		Trust	
Commitment	*Mutuality*	*Transparency*	*Trust*
Behavioural commitment	Affective commitment	Honesty	Blind trust
Benevolence	Calculated commitment	Social bonding	Credibility
Continuance commitment	Mutual understanding	Forward-looking intention	Reliability
Inter-firm commitment	Cost reduction		
Investment in transaction-specific assets – forward-looking			
Investment in transaction-specific assets – buyer-specific assets			
Relationship hostage			

Table A2.2   Innovative creativity dimensions and constructs

Creativity		Communication	Co-operation
Adaptation	*Innovation*		
Adaptability	Ability to innovate	Advisory communication	Marketing co-operation
Adaptive commitment	Creativity	Communication process	Shared responsibility
	Consistency	Conflict avoidance	Flexibility
		Information-sharing	Self-improvement
		Open communication	Joint planning
		Relevant communication	
		Responsive communication	
		Sales co-operation	
		Timely and accurate communication	

Table A2.3   Value creation and capture dimensions and constructs

Productive synergy		Value capture	Efficiency
Conflict management	*Synergy*		
Fairness	Compatible objectives	CLalt (brand)	HPOE
Conflict resolution	Stated objectives	CLalt (product)	KPI (Admin)
Functional conflict		CLalt (profitability)	KPI (SLA)
Manifest conflict		Profit-sharing	Metric effectiveness
			Performance measurement
			Quality improvement (operational)

For each of the constructs in Tables A2.1–A2.3, we can determine a series of measures as detailed below; we would typically use a seven- or ten-point Likert scale (Agree–Disagree):

- **Ability to innovate** – The relationship encourages us to be innovative and flexible in the way we do business.

- **Adaptability** – There is a willingness to adapt products, procedures, inventory, management, attitudes, values and goals to the needs of the relationship.

- **Adaptive commitment** – Such is the goodwill in the relationship, the other party would willingly put him/herself out to adapt to our changing requirements.

- **Advisory communication** – We provide the other party with regular information including long-range up to date forecasts and market developments to enable him to do his business better.

- **Affective commitment** – I have common goals with the other party and I see them as a business partner.

- **Behavioural commitment** – We provide special aid to this supplier when it is in trouble.

- **Benevolence** – The other party demonstrably supports my business development.

- **Benevolence (Alt)** – The other party is dedicated to making our partnership a success.

- **Benevolence (Alt)** – The other party is genuinely concerned that our business succeeds.

- **Blind trust** – We trust the other party to always act in our best interests.

- **Calculated commitment** – The overall contribution to my business of the other party makes it important that the relationship continues.

- **Calculated commitment (Alt)** – The relationship provides a dynamic business environment within which both parties can seek increasing rewards.

- **CLalt (brand)** – In comparison with our main supplier the strength of the other party's brand significantly helps generate sales.

- **CLalt (product)** – In comparison with our main supplier the features and functionality of the other party products make them easy for me to sell.

- **CLalt (profitability)** – In comparison with our main supplier the pricing and rebates of the other party's products to me make them profitable for me to sell.

- **Communication process** – We would welcome a shared data environment where market, planning, technical and pricing information are made freely available.

- **Compatible objectives** – The objectives of both parties are fully compatible.

- **Conflict avoidance** – We are aware of the performance requirements for all participants in the supply chain from suppliers to customers.

- **Conflict resolution** – Disagreements, if they occur, are resolved quickly and smoothly.

- **Conflict resolution (Alt)** – Disputes and problems are resolved quickly.

- **Consistency** – The other party is reliable and consistent in dealing with us.

- **Continuance commitment** – I see my relationship with the other party as important to the longer-term growth of my company.

- **Continuance commitment (Alt)** – We believe that this relationship is so important as to warrant maximum effort to maintain it.

- **Co-operation overview** – Both parties co-operate wholeheartedly.

- **Cost reduction** – The other party provides us with useful cost reduction and quality improvement ideas.

- **Creativity** – The relationship encourages us to be innovative and creative in the way we do business.

- **Credibility** – I have belief in the other party's ability to deliver on what they have told me they plan to do.

- **Fairness** – Disputes and problems are resolved fairly.

- **Flexibility** – The other party helps me out in whatever way we ask.

- **Forward-looking intention** – I have complete confidence in the intentions of the other party to make this partnership a success.

- **Functional conflict** – Any differences of opinion with the other party are simply treated as part of business.

- **Functional conflict (Alt)** – Problems are solved in a joint, open, constructive manner.

- **Functional conflict (Alt)** – When an unexpected problem arises, both parties would rather work out a solution than hold each other to the original contract terms.

- **Honesty** – The other party is always totally open and honest with us.

- **HPOE** (high-performance operating environment) – The relationship encourages the achievement of high performance by both parties (for example, consistent product quality, on-time delivery, reasonable forecasts).

- **Information-sharing** – Where the other party has proprietary information that could improve the performance of the joint business, it is freely available.

- **Inter-firm commitment** – We feel totally committed to this partnership.

- **Investment in transaction-specific assets – buyer-specific assets** – I have made significant investments in making my partnership with the other party work.

- **Investment in transaction-specific assets – forward-looking** – We are willing to invest more (money, time, information, effort) in the current relationship.

- **Investment in transaction-specific assets – supplier-specific assets** – The other party has made significant investment in ensuring our partnership with it is a success.

- **Joint planning** – We hold regular joint planning sessions with the other party.

- **KPI (Admin)** – The quality of service (for example, billing, prompt payment, administration, delivery) is entirely satisfactory.

- **KPI (SLA)** – The quality of the contract outputs (for example, service level agreement metrics) is entirely satisfactory.

- **Manifest conflict** – We have few serious disagreements with the other party.

- **Marketing co-operation** – The support provided through marketing programmes helps our business to grow.

- **Metric effectiveness** – Performance measurement is used to raise standards.

- **Mutual understanding** – The other party displays a sound, strategic understanding of our business.

- **Open communication** – The other party discusses its plans with me and listens to my comments.

- **Partnership performance** – Objective performance measurement is an important part of this relationship.

- **Profit-sharing** – The gains from this relationship are equally shared between both parties.

- **Quality improvement (Operational)** – The relationship is characterised by a continually improving product/service quality philosophy.

- **Quality improvement (Operational) (Alt)** – The relationship is characterised by a continually improving product quality philosophy.

- **Relationship hostage** – We are happy that our future is bound to the success of our relationship partner.

- **Relationship hostage (Alt)** – We do not feel 'imprisoned'/restricted within the current relationship.

- **Relevant communication** – The information provided about programmes and policies is relevant to my business.

- **Reliability** – The other party always lives up to its promises.

- **Reliability (Alt)** – The other party always does what it says it will do.

- **Responsive communication** – We understand the information requirements of all participants in the supply chain from suppliers to customers.

- **Sales co-operation** – We regularly receive good-quality sales leads from the other party.

- **Self-improvement** – Both sides are working to improve this relationship.

- **Shared responsibility** – The responsibility for making sure the relationship works is shared jointly.

- **Social bonding** – I have an excellent personal relationship with our account manager or main contact within the other party.

- **Social bonding (Alt)** – I have seen the generation of trust and openness through personal interaction.

- **Stated objectives** – The objectives of both parties are clearly stated.

- **Timely and accurate communication** – Information provided about products and services is timely and accurate.

- **Timely and accurate communication (Alt)** – Exchange of information in this relationship takes place frequently and informally, not just according to specified agreement.

Bibliography

Anderson, E. and Narus, J. (1991) 'Partnering as a Focused Marketing Strategy', *California Management Review* 33(3), 95–113.

Barney, J. (1991) 'Firm Resources and Sustained Competitive Advantage', *Journal of Management* 17(1), 99–120.

Beckman, C.M., Haunschild, P.R. and Phillips, D.J. (2004) 'Friends or Strangers? Firm-specific Uncertainty, Market Uncertainty, and Network Partner Selection', *Organisation Science* 15(3), May–June, 259–75.

Choi, T.Y and Hong, Y. (2002) 'Unveiling the Structure of Supply Networks: Case Studies in Honda, Acura, and DaimlerChrysler', *Journal of Operations Management* 20(5), 469–93.

Clark, M. (2002) 'The Relationship between Employees' Perceptions of Organisational Climate and Customer Retention Rates in a Major UK Retail Bank', *Journal of Strategic Marketing* 10, 93–113.

Cranfield School of Management (2007) 'Interview: Professor Martin Christopher. Logistics and Supply Chain Management: Creating Value Added Networks'. Bedford: Cranfield School of Management: www.som.cranfield.ac.uk/som/dinamic-content/media/knowledgeinterchange/booksummaries/Logistics%20and%20Supply%20Chain%20Management/Transcript.pdf (accessed 21 June 2012).

Cummins, T. (2010) 'The Role of Contracts and Commercial Management', in Humphries, A. and Gibbs, R. (eds) *Collaborative Change: Creating High Performance Partnerships and Alliances*. Charleston, SC: CreateSpace.

Dahlem, A. (2012) *Open Innovation, Networks and Strategic Partnerships in Drug Discovery and Development*. Indianapolis, IN: Eli Lilly & Co.: http://fnih.org/sites/all/files/documents/Andrew_Dahlem.pdf (accessed 14 February 2014).

Davis, E.W. and Spekman, R.E. (2003) *The Extended Enterprise: Gaining Competitive Advantage through Collaborative Supply Chains*. London: Financial Times/Prentice Hall.

Deal, T.E. and Kennedy, A.A. (1982) *Corporate Cultures: The Rites and Rituals of Corporate Life*. Harmondsworth: Penguin Books.

Dong, L. and Glaister, K. (2007) 'National and Corporate Culture Differences in International Strategic Alliances: Perceptions of Chinese Partners', *Asia Pacific Journal of Management* 25, 191–205.

Doz, Y. and Hamel, G. (1998) *Alliance Advantage: The Art of Creating Value through Partnering*. Boston, MA: Harvard Business Press.

Doz, Y. and Hunter, M. (2003) *Fuji Xerox and the Xerox Corp: Turning Tables?* Case Reference no. 303-076-1. Wellesley, MA: INSEAD.

Dyer, J. and Singh, H. (1998) 'The Relational View: Competitive Strategy and Sources of Interorganizational Competitive Advantage', *Academy of Management Review* 23(4), 660–79.

Dyer, J., Kale, P. and Singh, H. (2001) 'How to Make Strategic Alliances Work', *Sloan Management Review* 42(4), 37–43.

Edmondson, A.C., Michael, A., Boehmer, R., Ferlins, E.M. and Feldman, L.R (2005) 'The Recovery Window: Organisational Learning Following Ambiguous Threats', in Starbuck, W.H. and Farjoun, M. (eds) *Organisation at the Limit*. London: Blackwell Publishing.

Galbreath, J. (2002) 'Success in the Relationship Age: Building Quality Relationship Assets for Market Value Creation', *The TQM Magazine* 14(1), 8–24.

Gattorna, J. (2006) *Dynamic Supply Chains: Delivering Value through People*. London: Financial Times/Prentice Hall.

Gibbs, R. and Humphries, A. (2009) *Strategic Alliances and Marketing Partnerships: Gaining Competitive Advantage through Collaboration and Partnering*. London: Kogan Page.

Goffee, R. and Jones, G. (1996) 'What Holds the Modern Company Together?', *Harvard Business Review*, November–December, 133–58.

Goleman, D., Boyatzis, R. and Mckee, A. (2004) *Primal Leadership: Learning to Lead With Emotional Intelligence*. Boston, MA: Harvard Business Review Press.

Gomes-Casseres, B. (1996) *The Alliance Revolution: The New Shape of Business Rivalry*. Cambridge, MA: Harvard University Press.

Gomes-Casseres, B. (1997) 'Competing in Constellations: The Case of Fuji Xerox', *Strategy Business* 6, First Quarter, 4–16: www.strategy-business.com/article/8969 (accessed 18 March 2014).

Gomes-Casseres, B. and McQuade K. (1991) *Xerox and Fuji Xerox*. Case 9-391-156. Boston, MA: Harvard Business School.

Handy, C. (1985) *Understanding Organisations*. Harmondsworth: Penguin Books.

Hawkins, D.E. (2010) 'Collaboration: An Imperative for the Future', in Humphries, A. and Gibbs, R. (eds) *Collaborative Change: Creating High Performance Partnerships and Alliances*. Charleston, SC: CreateSpace.

Hawkins, D.E (2013) *Raising the Standard for Collaboration: Harnessing the Benefits of BS 11000, Collaborative Business Relationships*. London: BSI Standards Ltd.

Hofstede G. (2001) *Culture's Consequences: Comparing Values, Behaviours, Institutions, and Organisations across Nations*. London: Sage Publications.

House, R.J., Hanges, P., Javidan, M., Dorfman, P. and Gupta, V. (2000) *Culture, Leadership, and Organizations: The GLOBE Study of 62 Societies*. Thousand Oaks, CA: Sage Publications.

Humphries, A. and Gibbs, R. (2010) *Collaborative Change: Creating High Performance Partnerships and Alliances*. Charleston, SC: CreateSpace.

Humphries, A. and McComie, L. (2010) 'Performance Measurement in the Management of Food Supply Chain Relationships', in Mena, C. and Stevens, G. (eds) *Delivering Performance in Food Supply Chains*. Cambridge: Woodhead Publishing.

Humphries, A. and McComie, L. (2014a) *Contracts or Relationships: What's Right for Collaborative Enterprises?* Milton Keynes: SCCI: www.sccindex.com/Documents/Contracts%20or%20Relational%20Governancel%20the%20right%20choice.pdf (accessed 6 September 2014).

Humphries, A. and McComie, L. (2014b) *Implementing and Managing Collaborative Relationships: A Simple Guide*, 3rd edn. Milton Keynes: SCCI.

Humphries, A. and McComie, L. (2014c) *Is Collaboration Value a Mirage?* Milton Keynes: SCCI: www.sccindex.com/Documents/Is%20Collaboration%20Value%20a%20Mirage%20-%20March%20%202014.pdf (accessed 6 September 2014).

Hwang, P. and Burgers, W.P. (1997) 'The Many Faces of Multi-firm Alliances: Lessons for Managers', *California Management Review* 39(3), 101–17.

International Association for Contract and Commercial Management (2012) *The Future of Contracting.* London: IACCM: www.ariba.com/assets/uploads/documents/The+Future+of+Contracting-5-15-2012.pdf (accessed 6 September 2014).

Koka, B.R., Madhavan, R. and Prescott, J.E. (2006) 'The Evolution of Interfirm Networks: Environmental Effects on Patterns of Network Change', *Academy of Management Review* 31(3), 721–37.

Kumar, N. (1996) 'The Power of Trust in Manufacturer–retailer Relationships', *Harvard Business Review*, November–December, 92–106.

Lewin, A.Y. and Peeters, C. (2006) 'Offshoring Work: Business Hype or the Onset of Fundamental Transformation?', *Long Range Planning* 39(3), 211–39.

Mahnke, V., Overby, M.L. and Vang, J. (2005) 'Strategic Outsourcing of IT Services: Theoretical Stocktaking and Empirical Challenges', *Industry and Innovation* 12(2), 205–53.

Market & Business Development (2014) *UK Facilities Management Market Research Report.* London: MBD.

McGrath, R. (2013) *The End of Competitive Advantage.* Boston, MA: Harvard Business Review Press.

Mena, C., Humphries, A. and Choi, T. (2013) 'Toward a Theory of Multi-tier Supply Chain Management', *Journal of Supply Chain Management* 49(2), 58–77.

Nevin, M. (2014) *The Strategic Alliance Handbook: A Practitioners Guide to Business-to-business Collaborations.* Farnham: Gower Publishing.

Overby, M.K. (2005) *Partner Selection Criteria in Strategic Alliances: When to Ally with Weak Partners*. Paper presented at DRUID Academy PhD Winter 2005 Conference: www.druid.dk/conferences/winter2005/papers/dw2005-304.pdf (accessed 20 August 2010).

Parry, K. and Bryman, A. (2006) 'Leadership in Organizations', in Clegg, S., Hardy, C., Lawrence, T. and Nord, T (eds) *The Sage Handbook of Organization Studies*, 2nd edn. London. Sage Publications.

Pathak, S.D., Day, J., Nair, A., Sawaya, W. and Kristal, M. (2007) 'Complexity and Adaptivity in Supply Networks: Building Supply Network Theory Using a Complex Adaptive Systems Perspective', *Decision Sciences* 38(4), 547–80.

Perie, R. (2008) 'All for One: Factors for Alignment of Inter-dependent Businesses at KLM and Schipol'. PhD thesis, Technische Universitate Delft.

Poppo, L. and Zenger, T. (2002) 'Do Formal Contracts and Relational Governance Function as Substitutes or Complements?', *Strategic Management Journal* 23(8), 707–25.

Porter, M.E. (1985) *The Competitive Advantage: Creating and Sustaining Superior Performance*. New York: Free Press.

Porter, M.E. (1998) *Competitive Strategy: Techniques for Analyzing Industries and Competitors*. New York: Free Press.

Prahalad, C.K. and Hamel, G. (1998) 'The Core Competence of the Corporation', *Harvard Business Review*, May–June, 79–90.

Prahalad, C.K. and Ramaswamy, V. (2000) 'Co-opting Customer Competence', *Harvard Business Review*, January–February, 79–87.

Quinn, J.B. and Hilmer, F.G. (1994) 'Strategic Outsourcing', *Sloan Management Review* 35, 43–55.

Rumelt, R. (1991) 'How Much Does Industry Matter?', *Strategic Management Journal* 12, 167–85.

Samuel, A. (2012) 'The Social Solution to Innovation Challenges', *Harvard Business Review Blog Network*, 11 December: http://blogs.hbr.org/2012/12/the-social-solution-to-busines/ (accessed 11 December 2013).

Sanchez, R., Heene, A. and Thomas, H. (1996) 'Towards the Theory and Practice of Competence-based Competition', in Sanchez, R., Heene, A. and Thomas, H. (eds) *Dynamics of Competence-based Competition*. Oxford: Elsevier Pergamon.

Simpson, P., Siguaw, J. and Baker, T. (2001) 'A Model of Value Creation: Supplier Behaviors and their Impact on Retailer Perceived Value', *Industrial Marketing Management* 30, 119–34.

Tate, W.L. and Ellram, L.M. (2009) 'Offshore Outsourcing: A Managerial Framework', *Journal of Business and Industrial Marketing* 24(3/4), 256–68.

Tuckman, B. (1965) 'Developmental Sequence in Small Groups', *Psychological Bulletin* 63(6), 384–99.

Tuckman, B. and Jensen, M. (1977) 'Stages of Small-group Development Revisited', *Group Organization Management* 2(4), 419–27.

Wilding, R. and Humphries, A. (2006) 'Understanding Collaborative Supply Chain Relationships through the Application of the Williamson Organisation Failure Framework', *International Journal of Physical Distribution and Logistics Management* 36(4), 309–29.

Wilding, R. and Humphries, A. (2009) 'Building Relationships that Create Value', in Gattorna, J. (ed.) *Dynamic Supply Chain Alignment*. Farnham: Gower Publishing.

Williamson, O.E. (1975) *Markets and Hierarchies: Analysis and Anti-trust Implications*. New York: The Free Press.

Xerox (2010) *Xerox Annual Report 2009*: www.xerox.com/annual-report-2009/xerox-business/fuji-xerox.html (accessed 22 January 2011).

Xerox (2011) *Xerox Annual Report 2010*: www.xerox.com/annual-report-2010/xerox-business/fuji-xerox.html (accessed 1 April 2014).

Zirpoli, F. and Becker, M.C. (2011) 'What Happens When You Outsource Too Much?', *Sloan Management Review* 52(2), 59–64.

Index

For Product Safety Concerns and Information please contact our EU representative GPSR@taylorandfrancis.com Taylor & Francis Verlag GmbH, Kaufingerstraße 24, 80331 München, Germany

Printed and bound by CPI Group (UK) Ltd, Croydon, CR0 4YY

01/05/2025

01858368-0005